Endorsements

"I can explain this book in five words: "Go extreme or go home." The choice between awesomeness and mediocrity is yours to make. If you choose awesomeness, then Carter has provided the path for you."

Guy Kawasaki
Chief evangelist of Canva and Mercedes-Benz
brand ambassador

"Sandy Carter is a true expert in innovation who clearly lays out the roadmap for innovators struggling to find a way forward. She provides deep yet easily digestible insights for all, including individual entrepreneurs or corporations. Her advice is timely, especially as the world moves forward at lightning speed."

Anna Shen
Huffington Post

"*Extreme Innovation* is not an option. When you examine the speed of change, it pales by comparison to the speed of technology innovation. Sandy Carter was at the leading edge of Social Innovation, and continues her legacy in this powerful and impactful book. Reading *Extreme Innovation* will startle you and inspire you – Putting *Extreme Innovation* into practice will capture and sustain leadership and wealth."

Jeffrey Gitomer
Author of *The Little Red Book of Selling*

"This exhaustively researched book is very well done and holds a ton of information about Extreme Innovation. I love the fact that Sandy talks about technology's impact as well as the fact that diversity drives innovation. As a business leader, I know that innovation will be a make or break for most companies going forward."

Vaishali Kasture
Partner Deloitte India Consulting – Head of Robotics Practice

"Exceptional - up to date, well researched (time with startups and companies vs just "theory"), and truly engaging (couldn't put it down)! Innovation is the lifeblood of entrepreneurs."

Sanjay Mehta
Top Angel Investor With 60+Companies portfolio

"Reading your book is like a bolt of lightning. A surge of power and passion! Your inspiration has sparked new ideas around my own project. You are luminous in this brave, new world. And the world needs bright, bright Lights now more than ever."

Dr. Elizabeth Lindsey
Explorer, National Geographic, Anthropologist, Extreme Innovator

"Sandy Carter brings the 'superpowers' that underpin extreme innovation into crisp view in this well-timed book. *Extreme Innovation* demystifies Silicon Valley's innovation black box. Sandy Carter provides a roadmap to fast-forward companies and their leaders to the innovation future. Her grounded and easily digestible advice is anchored in the pillars of extreme innovation--intelligence, speed and synergy. *Extreme Innovation* can be applied *today* by companies choosing to innovate to generate profit and growth."

Mary B. Teagarden
Professor of Global Strategy, Thunderbird School of Global Management at Arizona State University

"Extreme Innovation is.... a book to be embraced, studied, and implemented."

Amy Wilkinson
CEO of Ingenuity and author of *The Creator's Code*

"As a Director and professor in the Integrated Innovation Institute at Carnegie Mellon University, I see innovation and new product creation speeding up continuously. The harnessing of innovation to address the challenges of our societies is critical. CMU partnered with Sandy Carter on the research for "Extreme Innovation" around female founders in order to understand these extreme innovators and share the findings. The superpowers of intelligence, speed, and synergy are the skills required for our rapidly changing world. Every executive should read and study these insights."

Sheryl Root
Director, MS in Technology Ventures, Carnegie Mellon University

"Sandy gives you the recipe for keeping your business relevant and thriving in a world that's about to see tremendous technological change thanks to AI, mixed reality, IoT advances, autonomous cars, robots drones, crypto currency, and much more."

Robert Scoble
Evangelist at Upload VR and co-author of *The Fourth Transformation*

"While information is plentiful, insight is invaluable. Rich in content and context, Sandy Carter's unique perspective can bring a disruptively powerful fuel and force to those who are bold enough to embrace, adopt and implement Extreme Innovation principles. What will you choose?"

Sara Hand
CEO Spark Growth and Visionary Leader of 3.0
Leaders Innovation and Investment Conference

"There are a great many books written about Silicon Valley, its culture and ways of succeeding. Few endure for more than a few months. Sandy Cutler's *Extreme Innovation* is one of the few that will endure for years. It is an important book, a guide for entrepreneurs and corporate CEOs to navigate forward in the turbulent times."

Shel Israel
Partner, Transformation Group

"Looking for unparalleled innovation and improvements to the way your organization operates? In *Extreme Innovation*, Sandy Carter demonstrates how leveraging powerful new technology, new world ecosystems including the impact of social sales and marketing, and cognitive diversity will transform your business into an extreme innovation hub."

Jill Rowley
Chief Evangelist #SocialSelling & Startup Advisor, Top 10 Influencer in Social Selling

"The rapid evolution of XR (VR/AR/MR) is going to massively influence how we interact with technology, each other, and the world around us, for years to come. *Extreme Innovation* easily describes how these technologies impact the brave new world of innovation."

Dave Curry
VP Emerging Trends & Technology, POP

"*Extreme Innovation* is an awesome book because it is relevant to all businesses. innovation means different things to different people, and is often context specific. For example, innovation within Facebook's software is totally different than innovation for the 49ers offensive line. Therefore, I love this book because it helps ask the right questions to get you to a business outcome of profit and purpose."

Geoff De Weaver
Chief Executive Officer + Founder at TouchPoint Entertainment Inc.

"Through stories and clear frameworks, *Extreme Innovation* teaches you the superpowers you need to spark and foster innovation. A must-have playbook for today's business leaders."

Ekaterina Walter
Business Innovator, International Speaker, Author of WSJ Bestselling book *Think Like Zuck*

"Sandy Carter promises brilliant insight and delivers. Her focus on using technologies like artificial intelligence (AI), bots and cognitive diversity as keys to innovation is thought provoking. As a CEO of a company that focuses on connecting Fortune 500 companies with innovative technologies, I know the power AI and bots bring to innovation. Whether you are an innovator – startup or a corporate executive wanting to grow with extreme innovation, you must read this book!"

Adelyn Zhou
CEO, TOPBOTS

"It took Elon Musk only 6 days to push a software update to tens of thousands of cars based on my tweet. Speed is the most important quality of startups. Learn this super power and more in Sandy Carter's extraordinary book *Extreme Innovation*."

Loic Le Meur
Founder Leade.rs and Le Web

Extreme Innovation

3 Superpowers for Purpose and Profit

Sandy Carter

PARAM MEDIA INC.
Vancouver, BC

ISBN 978-0-9950302-7-5

Front cover art by Paul Stadnyk at Revved Design
and Param Media

ParamMedia.com
SandyCarter.net

Dedicated to my loving family:

Todd, Maria, Kassie, and parents Dorothy and Ray.

Acknowledgements

Param Media—thank you to the Param Media team, who were true extreme innovators and worked miracles on the book. They were professional, and as passionate as I was about the book—even during snow storms!

Anna Shen—to my friend and lady in red, Anna Shen, contributor at Huffington Post and Fortune. Thank you for reviewing every chapter of the book and for your magical writing assistance. I appreciated the encouragement and daily calls that kept me motivated throughout the process.

Tamara McCleary—thank you for being an angel of encouragement and knowledge. I am so thankful that we bonded at that infamous Elton John concert! This quote makes me think of you: "Good friends are like angels, You don't have to see them to know they are there for you."

Michael Pokocky—thank you for sharing your magic touch in writing, and for contributing that magic in several chapters to help me weave the story.

Gary Spirer—thank you for sharing the gift of writing, research, and insight as a successful CEO.

Paul Stadnyk—thank you for surprising me with your great additional design on the cool book cover!

Robert Davis—many thanks for helping to shape my thinking in Extreme Innovation and the superpowers!

Many thanks also for my innovation experts who shared their expertise, including:

Tiffani Bova, Brian Buntz, Brian Fanzo, Erby Foster, Diane Flynn, Adriana Gascoigne, Melissa Hargis, Anina Net, Shel

Israel, Rob May, Tamara McCleary, Monique Morrow, Jeremiah Owyang, Amanda Richardson, Raj Setty, Brian Solis, Gary Spierer, the SmartVizx Team—Monami Mitra, Kunal Grover, Gautam Tewari, and Tithi Tewari, and Allison Wiener.

Thank you to the following groups for leading edge research on extreme innovation, including:

Carnegie Mellon Silicon Valley—Neha Goyal, Eileen Wei, and Simrata Gandhi, Julie Meyer and Ariadne Capital, Professor Henry Chesbrough, Boston Consulting Group, Brian Solis, Altimeter, and Cap Gemini, Jeremiah Owyang, Booz and Company, ScienceDirect, Product Innovation Journal, Tech Pro Research, CrispIdea Research, Digi-Capital, the Harvard Business Review, McKinsey, Wharton Professor Peter Cappelli, former AARP CEO Bill Novelli, City University of London's Cass Business School, Accenture, Deloitte, Carnegie Mellon, Pew Research, Endeavor Insight, Forbes—The World's Most Innovative Companies, Professor Rita Gunther McGrath, Forrester Research, Ariadne Capital, the University of California, the Stanford Graduate School of Business, *Good to Great* by Jim Collins, *Who Moved My Cheese* by Spencer Johnson, other research in books like *The Essential Bennis* by Warren Bennis and Patricia Ward Biederman, and *Leading Change* by John P. Kotter, The Fourth Transformation, USC Lava Lab, BNP Paribas Global Entrepreneur Report, Eileen Clegg, Intel's latest research, "Decoding Diversity: The Financial and Economic Returns in Tech," and so many more.

Thanks to over 50 examples of extreme innovators, including:

RayBaby, Regeneron, Tesla, Adobe, Uber, Lyft, Google, Amazon, Microsoft, MasterCard, Shake Shack, Barclaycard, LEGO, Quantas Airlines, ESPN, Snap, Sandcreek Middle School, Siemens, Renfe, GM, littleBits, Hatch Baby, Urban 3D, CarForce, suitX, Atipica, 6sense, Cisco, Talla, Betaworks, Lowe's, TOMS, Apple, Facebook, Bitcoin, Follow My Vote, Vault OS, Slock.it, BTCJam, Domino's, Under Armour, Veeva Systems, Twilio, Box, Wealthfront, Baidu, SXSW, Trello, and WFFConnect.

Thank you to over 71 experts who gave their time for in person interviews, and who represent a variety of organizations, including:

Hotel Tonight, Salesforce, Clorox, SmartVizx, Betagig, Crowd Companies, Swissnex, Sephora, Girls in Tech, Semios, ReBoot Accel, JetBlue, iSocialFanz, MentorCloud, Thulium, 360Fashion Network, Intel, DilogR, AiNGEL, Silicon Blitz, plus interviews with 51 female founders.

TABLE OF CONTENTS

FOREWORD 1

——

FOREWORD 2

——

CHAPTER 1
Extreme Innovation 5

——

CHAPTER 2
Shhhhh! Secrets from the Bay Area 27

——

CHAPTER 3
The New Superpowers 39

——

CHAPTER 4
Super Intelligence: Cutting Edge Explorer 47

——

CHAPTER 5
Super Intelligence: Data Hunger Driven by IoT
and Social Media 67

CHAPTER 6

Super Intelligence: Artificial Intelligence
and Bots 85

———

CHAPTER 7

Super Intelligence with VR/AR as Innovation
Accelerators 95

———

CHAPTER 8

Super Intelligence using Blockchain 109

———

CHAPTER 9

Super Speed: Cognitive Diversity 119

———

CHAPTER 10

Super Speed: Continuous Learning Culture of
Mentoring 145

———

CHAPTER 11

Super Synergy: Customer Obsession 157

———

CHAPTER 12

Super Synergy: Ecosystems 171

CHAPTER 13
Super Synergy: The Connections between
Marketing, Sales, and Service 183

___

CHAPTER 14
Extreme Innovator Traits 193

___

CHAPTER 15
The Superpower Assessment 205

___

CHAPTER 16
Opening the Way for Female Entrepreneurs
and Intraprenuers 213

___

CHAPTER 17
Super Powerful Advice 227

EPILOGUE 235

EXTREME GLOSSARY 237

ENDNOTES 251

FOREWORD 1

Dr. Elizabeth Lindsey
Explorer, National Geographic,
Anthropologist, Extreme Innovator

This is the **epic foreword to a truly epic book**. When I finished reading *Extreme Innovation*, I knew I had read an extraordinary manuscript. Why does innovation matter to me – the first Polynesian Explorer and female Fellow in the history of the National Geographic Society? Because I am an extreme explorer who had to innovate throughout the world. Look around. How many of the innovations that we know today actually came from a world explorer? Some say what I do is pure magic – I know it as extreme innovation.

Innovation is important in all fields, not just technology, and all over the world, not just Silicon Valley. It is constantly changing, just like the environment I explore. Studying the superpowers required in the brave new world, and being gifted with proven frameworks to help companies capture their power, is invaluable. Like explorers, innovators are groundbreakers. Because of that, they must go beyond the boundaries of today's knowledge and discover a new way. This book shares over 100 examples of those who have led the way. Learn from them, and experiment for yourself in your own culture.

I am currently developing technology to conserve and safeguard cultural wisdom and knowledge. Sandy has captured the power of these next gen technologies to innovate, whether it is through artificial intelligence or virtual reality. Exploring these areas and their potential, empowers the soul of extreme innovation. It is usable and real.

As a believer in diversity of thought, I often say "In a society that celebrates youth, we have forsaken the wisdom of age." Combining the power of millennials, with those more experienced, women, men, and representatives of every type of diversity, drives innovation. While it is proven in the research shared in this book, I have witnessed it in full measure among navigator-priests, from Micronesia to mystics in India. I applaud Sandy for raising its impact on innovation.

Extreme innovation amplifies the culture required to change the status quo. It is that culture, those secrets, that drive me to conserve, learn, and share. So fellow explorers – extreme innovators – celebrate this brave new world, a world that needs a new kind of extreme innovator, a world that needs you to create the culture required to nourish the next generation.

Enjoy this book, soak in its wisdom and knowledge, and apply it to your life.

Be an extreme innovator.

Dr. Elizabeth Lindsey

FOREWORD 2

Robert Scoble
Evangelist at Upload VR and co-author of
The Fourth Transformation:
How AI and AR will change everything

I am extreme when it comes to seeing the next thing and pushing it to its limits. I mean I wore Google glasses in the shower in 2013, and of course, had to do it again with Snap Spectacles. That passion for new technologies, products, and companies, has gotten me a ton of firsts in my life. Elon Musk gave me the first ride in the first Tesla before he gave his best friend one. Siri was launched in my son's bedroom. I've seen thousands of startups before anyone else, from Pandora to Flipboard.

Channel 9 for Microsoft was started by me and four other guys, in big part based on my innovator DNA. And I was first to predict the next transformation, or change in interface, if you will, as our industry moves to a new form of augmented reality, that overlays virtual items and worlds on top of the real world, which Microsoft and I call "mixed reality."

We are on the cusp of a great innovation inflection point like never before due to that, but lots of other things. AI. Autonomous drones, cars, trucks, and robots. Smart cities with fields of devices enabled by IoT. Innovation just began a whole new cycle.

Foreword

Now businesses don't need to just worry about how they will innovate on physical products and brand identity, but virtual ones too. Your customers will soon demand it, thanks to new lightweight glasses that will arrive in 2018. By 2020 your business will need to be augmented, and that's just the start. Mercedes told me that sometime between 2020 and 2025 we will get a true level 5 autonomous car – one that can drive around without a human in it.

Extreme Innovation is a book that serves up this defining moment in time. It shows how to use new tech to create super intelligence, and ecosystems to create super synergies, and why diversity of thought – or cognitive diversity – ignites innovation with super speed.

You're going to need the recipes laid out here to get your business ready for this new virtual + real world that's coming quickly.

You should give this book to some of your colleagues and business associates. Rip the pages out to tack up on your walls, copy the frameworks to guide you through the innovation journey. Not only did Sandy do her own research with Carnegie Mellon Silicon Valley, she leveraged research from her tribe around the world – the latest in the industry.

Play. Experiment. Call me if you need Mixed reality help, and damn it, Sandy, not only are you a badass but you wrote an awesome book too that businesses need to deliver what's next!

Robert Scoble

CHAPTER 1
Extreme Innovation

Are you an extreme innovator?

How you answer this question can change your life forever.

I am a business executive who is a natural networker, innovator, and an avid social media evangelist. So it is fitting that I open this book with an example of innovation that started from a Twitter conversation involving the #1 rated innovative company: Tesla.[1]

This legendary tweet from my friend Loic Lc Mcur, Founder of Leade.rs, LeWeb, and five other startups, was tweeted out to the CEO of Tesla, who has over 7M followers. It said simply: "the San Mateo supercharger is always full with idiots who leave their Tesla for hours even though it is already charged." And Elon Musk Tweeted back: "You're right, this is becoming an issue...Will take action." And action was taken in a super speed way. The headline from OfficeChai was: "Elon Musk Receives Product Suggestion on Twitter, Tesla Implements It 6 Days Later."[2]

Loic was surprised and told me: "Sandy, it took Elon Musk only 6 days to push a software update to tens of thousands of cars and fix the problem. Speed is the most important quality of startups. The fact that Tesla can operate at this speed even though it's not a startup anymore is extraordinary."

Imagine for a moment that this was your company. Would you or your CEO take this bold action? How would your company handle such a suggestion that came in from—gasp—a customer, not from a strategy team? And even if the suggestion was put on the table, could you move this fast? Tesla made the change in six days. Some might say that Elon is a superhero.

Many of us have a favorite superhero, whether it's Superman, CatWoman, or Neo in *The Matrix*. Superheroes are not just for children; they are also important for adults. They represent an ideal that we would like to embody. But while we may not be able to fly or have x-ray vision—or innovate and implement a major solution in six days—we can achieve our own superhero abilities. In fact, to survive in today's world of business, we really do need to become superheroes.

Without the ability to innovate, your business is not likely to survive. But innovation alone is not enough; now we need to move to *extreme innovation*, which includes innovating much more quickly, and with greater disruptive power than ever before. The hero in this new story is the artist in you, without whom no innovation can take place.

Why is this extreme innovation different? In the last six months, I have been researching, attending classes, visiting innovation labs, doing my own research with Carnegie Mellon Silicon Valley, coding in hackathons, judging startup competitions, and talking to everyone I can in the famed Silicon Valley where I live. What I have discovered is that there is a sea change that has occurred.

Many aspects of innovation are still true, but there are massive, extreme changes in the way we get intelligence, the way we gain speed, and the synergy required to win. I saw it in our own research with Carnegie Mellon Silicon Valley.

The Lily Pad Anomaly

I felt compelled to write this book to show you how the equation for innovation was being rewritten in the extreme. For example, when I was doing my research, the great innovation books didn't discuss using Virtual Reality (VR) or Blockchain in the usual innovative cycle, because they weren't around when those books were written. Cognitive diversity has also just emerged, and ecosystems are in their infancy. Things are changing. Fast.

Have you ever seen that brain teaser about the lily pads? I was reminded of it while at the Launch Scale conference listening to Rob May, founder of Talla.

(Source: Jay Castor)

The riddle goes like this. A lily pad doubles in size every day. If on the sixtieth day the pond is filled with lily pads, on what day is the pond only half covered? Since it doubles every day, and if the pond is half full on the fifty-ninth day, then it is filled on the sixtieth day. I don't want you to wait until day 59 to see these changes. I want you to move now!

Chapter 1

Get ready to grasp and be inspired by the ideas and information presented in this book, because extreme innovation is the only way for the hero—which is you—to have hope for the future of your business. It doesn't matter what industry you are in, because once you become your own superhero, there will be a much greater chance for you and your business to evolve at a previously unimaginable rate.

Extreme Innovation is combining new superpowers of intelligence, speed, and synergy to recognize, create, and jump on these new changes — the lily pads — with lightning speed.

I hope that this book also ignites the dreamer in you—someone who imagines the possibilities that can emerge once you are armed with new knowledge and a systematic approach to extreme innovation. If you truly embrace the messages in this book and understand what is possible, then you will be doing everything within your control to build your business in a market that has become highly complex, yet full of profound potential for a new success unlike anything we have ever seen before.

Innovation often requires many ideas coming together from various people. That's why I have included expert advice in the pages of this book. These experts or advisors come from a diverse set of backgrounds: large companies, startups, academia, and publishing. They all add different but equally important viewpoints on innovation from the Bay Area and beyond. Also, I did an original research project with Carnegie Mellon Silicon Valley about innovation with global female founders and entrepreneurs, including interviewing over 50 founders in person to gain innovative insight.

On this journey we will take together to becoming extreme innovators, the motivation is both purpose and profit. Contributing to making the world a better place is the goal for all of us. It's about your voice being heard, and how to stand out in a very crowded marketplace.

Consider me your personal mentor. I invite you to travel with me from the relative safety of your current life to become an extreme innovator. Let me know your thoughts on Twitter, LinkedIn, or Facebook.

So buckle up and let's go!

The Elevator Pitch

In a recent CEO study by PricewaterhouseCoopers, 93% of CEOs reported that innovation is the only way to grow their business. But 75% reported that they didn't believe their organizations could stay ahead of the latest trends in innovation.[3] This is profoundly concerning.

Although innovation is hip and cool and is one of the top buzzwords in the market, few are successfully executing it. Businesses must first understand innovation, and then deploy resources to achieve successful innovation. Companies increase their chances of being able to innovate if they apply the resources to figuring out which innovations can and should be implemented to give them the advantage to win.

Capital expenditure in innovation should be one of the top investments companies make. Why? I am in Silicon Valley, where there are various entrepreneur pitch competitions every day. In fact, on meetups alone, there are over

1,000 entrepreneur groups. Imagine this duplicated all over the world—from London to Lisbon, from Dublin to Dubai.

I recently returned from an entrepreneur pitch competition where top startups from all over the world presented their big ideas to the judges to disrupt and change the world—in artificial intelligence, drones, automotive, and wellness. The buzz in the room was palpable. Where there is excitement, at least in Silicon Valley, capital usually follows. Investors who are early adaptors see the big opportunities.

I also recently attended a large industry conference where the organizers announced innovative new products and changes to their business models, as well as their views about crowdsourcing the most innovative ideas from their clients. At this gathering, the opportunity for investors and ideas to come together could mean only one thing: success.

Everyone wants innovation, but executives generally have no roadmap to follow that is new and up to date. I found over 44 innovation models but none that reflected AI, Cognitive Diversity, or Ecosystems. That is why it is critical to share insights, best practices, and knowledge: to drive business outcomes with profit and purpose. That's why I want to share with you what you need to understand about extreme innovation, so that you can help your organization drive business outcomes.

Extreme Innovation is a Make or Break

In today's world, disruption is a foregone conclusion. Today's leaders must disrupt themselves and their industry or be disrupted. The idea of survival of the fittest and most adaptable is more vital now than ever.

As disruption in given markets becomes more widespread, today's businesses and workers will need to accelerate their pace of change. Those who do not adapt will die out. Common predictions note this will happen at a **faster rate** than that witnessed in the industrial age. The technological age is currently all about disruption and the pace of technological advancement is staggeringly fast.

Innovation—or a lack of innovation—is why, out of the top 10 companies by market capitalization in 2006, only three made the list a decade later.[4] These three companies that had staying power also had extreme innovation in their products, business models, and operations, as well as customer experience. Imagine seven companies being disrupted and coming off the list, only to be replaced by seven new businesses leveraging digital and technology to disrupt the original base of perceived strongholds.

The three who remained on the list survived because of extreme innovation and disruption to their own business models.

My prediction is that the next decade will require even more innovation—but not innovation in silos. What is needed now is a new innovation equation. What we need is extreme innovation. Think about Peter on the TV show *Family Guy*: he is always innovating some idea to please his wife Lois. That guy is extreme.

Extreme innovation is jumping on those lily pad elements early. It is about combining like we've never seen before. Super intelligence, super speed, and super synergy are

11

all about the brand new elements that will progress like those lily pads.

Let's take one example that you will learn about in this book: Artificial Intelligence (AI). It seems like it is slowly growing, but on day 59 you will realize its total impact. It has covered the pond.

Starting earlier in AI means you have an advantage. The more users you have leads to more data, which makes your app or bot smarter. This creates a sustainable advantage and provides you the ability to leverage extreme innovation for business growth.

GET A.I. ASAP

More users

More data

Smarter algorithms

Better product

(Revised image used with permission from
Rob May, CEO, Talla)

Company leadership may not engage in the same sort of antics shown on *Family Guy*, but companies certainly can whittle down their portfolio and reallocate funds for focusing on the extreme innovation part of their business. Often, this is the original core of their business that has become lost over time. Companies can lose their focus and deviate away from what their focus should be, such as leveraging back to growth by engaging with extreme innovation. These companies must now go back to the core of their business and come out of that process and grow with extreme innovation. A win will be secured for those teams that manage to do this.

It's also possible these businesses might invest in extreme innovator businesses to both enhance their current business and expand into new extreme innovator businesses. The possibilities require critical thinking and an understanding of what a business can and cannot control. It's like getting to know yourself again as you get older: because you have some wisdom and experiences to draw from, you can re-invent yourself and continue to live a prosperous life. The opposite of this idea is deciding to do nothing—but then you'll end up going to the grave full of regret.

Innovation is a Form of Empathy

For innovation to be real in your culture, it needs to be built on a foundation of the basics: people, process, and continually upgraded technology. We've always needed these basics, but now we must design agile processes and cultures, drive new technologies into everyone's business DNA, and build sustainable and scalable ecosystems.

If you have the superpowers on full power, empathy is the outcome. In a response to a blog I wrote, Tim Connor, a top micro venture capitalist, noted that empathy was the key he had seen in his successful companies.

Extreme innovation is not achieved alone; it is achieved in unity with partners, influencers, and customers or clients (these two words are often interchangeable). It is not envisioned just from the top, but is inclusive of the team. The millennial generation is bigger and more diverse than the boomers, and your team and the people they represent are a key to the future. Think about that one.

Extreme innovation leverages technology to the max, changing roles and context as necessary. To a great extent, it also integrates with, drives, or develops from technology. Recently, a group of thought leaders discussed how innovation within pre-existing systems must be done by stretching the limits of what's experimentally possible and experiential. New technology gives you new possibilities.

The three superpowers work in concert—technology and new ways of innovating require a people-driven culture that is cognitively diverse. Speed and synergy go hand in hand to create the next-level agile, continuous learning culture. In this book, we will go through all these concepts—so hold on tight! Below is the original concept drawn in true Silicon Valley style: on a napkin with a group of innovators over a meal in Palo Alto.

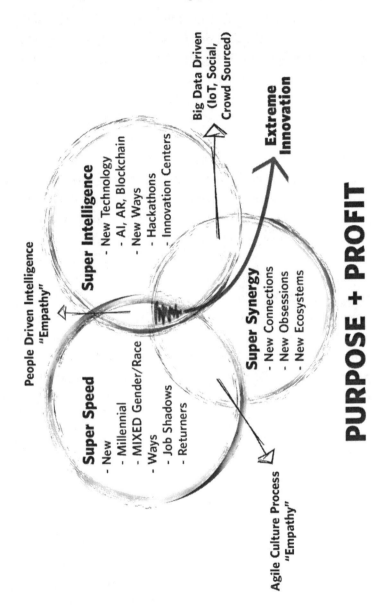

Furthermore, to survive new threats, and maximize new opportunities, three-stage innovation—people, process, and continuously upgraded technology—for companies requires new *superpowers* for leaders: *super intelligence, super speed*, and *super synergy*. I love watching the Justice League, a cartoon that originated in the 1960's where the superheroes all collaborated to save the world. In tomorrow's world, superpowers are required to disrupt, but it's crucial to note that collaboration is still required.

Brian Solis
Innovation Consultant, Altimeter

What Extreme Innovation is Not – Iteration

Consider the following historical moves.

- Kodak invested in film over digital early on even though the company was behind some of the first digital imaging patents and capabilities.
- Blockbuster rebuffed an acquisition offered by Netflix and thus missed the streaming revolution.
- The taxi industry at large chose volume over experience and innovation allowing for Uber, Lyft, and others to offer more attractive and relevant alternatives.
- Borders ended its marketing alliance with Amazon and instead decided to compete against it online.

Iteration vs. Extreme Innovation

Chapter 1

You can't move in a new direction if you don't lead the way. With every new technology, we witness the disruption of vulnerable businesses and even entire industries. Vulnerability however, is self-induced. Successful digital Darwinist strategies require action, risk, and experimentation to innovate. But, all too often, businesses default to risk-aversion and wind up confusing iteration with innovation. While both can be good for business, they are not the same. In fact, sometimes iteration can hinder acts of innovation, which ultimately affects to what extent a company progresses against digital Darwinism.

Key Terms:

- Iteration is doing the same things better.
- Innovation is doing new things that introduce new value.
- Disruption is doing new things that make the old ones obsolete

When I think about the evolution of business models and how companies invest in new technology to drive innovation, the traditional television remote control comes to mind. For starters, do you know anyone who actually enjoys the remote control experience? Neither do I. I often say that we have a reluctant relationship with our remotes.

So, if no one loves the remote, how is it that we got to this point? Well, it's a great example of iteration vs. innovation. Appreciating the differences will help us plan accordingly.

In my latest book, *X: The Experience When Business Meets Design*, I share a story of the evolution of the remote control complete with a custom infographic. I just had to know, "What happened?"

Over the last 60 or so years, remotes essentially were built upon previous foundations. Each generation tended to be better and more capable than the last, but never designed to challenge convention, consider user experience, or mirror how behaviors, gestures, and preferences/expectations were changing over time. The result is bolted-on tech stuffed into dated housing that delivers an awkward, dilapidated experience upon arrival.

Did you know that on average, remote controls have 70 buttons? In fact, the first smart phone apps designed to replace remotes looked and operated like the traditional bricks they were designed to replace. It's laughable considering that we live in a pinch, zoom, tap, swipe right kind of world these days.

This is iteration.

At the same time, these archaic bricks were designed to control innovative breakthroughs in TVs and set top boxes, the results of significant, ongoing R&D and innovation. If you think about it, TV screens today are ultra-thin with resolutions that rival the real world. Yet, the departments that design next-generation TVs are not collaborating with those cobbling together new-fangled remotes. Thus any product innovation in TVs is already compromised by the experience of having a reluctant relationship with the device that controls it.

Executives tend to think about new technology and possibilities the same way. They take the latest tech and build upon previous foundations often overlooking inherent relevance, agility, and ingenuity to do new things and create new value in the process.

This is a time for innovation.

Digital Transformation Takes Innovation and Iteration

Make no mistake. This is either going to happen to you or because of you. I'd like to believe it's the latter. The point though is that it's a choice. But, if you're waiting for someone to tell you what to do, where to go or how, you're on the wrong side of innovation.

To compete in an era of digital Darwinism takes a balance of innovation and iteration. You have to improve things. And, you must do new things that generate new value. Having a plan for both sets the stage for disruption, a gift worth giving, not getting. Everything must start, though, with the ability to see what others don't and do what others can't (or won't).

The way I see it, digital Darwinism isn't a threat. I believe it's an opportunity. More so, it's an invitation to innovate, to challenge convention, write a new set of rules, and to build a new infrastructure for business that makes the old models obsolete.

This is your legacy and it's yours to define. But, you can't change anything if you change nothing to do so. And, you can't move in a new direction if you don't lead the way. This is your time to pave the way for others to follow. It really is.

Extreme innovation is the way forward.

[Thanks Brian for your expert advice.]

Evolution of the Extreme Innovator

Building extreme innovator companies mirrors evolution in certain ways. To excel, companies must pull together physical technologies, social organization, and business processes that, as Eric D Beehacker notes, together "differentiate, select and amplify."[5]

Google innovated very powerfully by using data to differentiate, select favorable patterns, and amplify those that were most favorable, i.e. the most read and viewed, and those with the highest quality content, rating, and ranking. Then they applied an evolution-like data sorting model to their advertising model, matching content and their rankings based upon keywords, which they auctioned off depending on the demand for the keywords.

Google did not rely on the traditional scientific method of starting with a hypothesis and testing it to see whether the results came out as expected. Instead, the data evolved to the patterns that people revealed through use. Marketing, advertising, and all areas of business changed forever because Google was a disruptive extreme innovator.

Extreme innovators are found in companies that behave like Google. They are data-driven, and they have led the way to the data-driven technologies and disruptions they have developed.

Google co-founder Sergey Brin joined the director of the World Economic Forum (WEF) for a chat in January 2017. Sergey was asked about innovation, and he gave an example of what happens when someone comes to him and says something like, "I can put a chip in someone's eye." "Yeah, yeah," he responded to his engineer. "Go ahead and do it," he said, while waving his hand in the air like a king preoccupied with some other task. Later that same engineer came back to Sergey and said, "I did it." "Did what?" "I can put a chip in the eye of a person—but better than that, in contact lenses."

Then Sergey said to the director hosting the WEF chat that this idea, which he never gave a second thought to, has expanded into partnerships with manufacturers of contact lenses, and who knows what business products are going to come out of that innovation.

As part of understanding the process for allowing extreme innovation to flourish in your company, note how the co-founder of Google let the team go do it. He let them follow a creative path. This is a lesson for all CEOs and founders: to respect the artist in the culture of the company.

Extreme Innovator Technologies

All industries are fiercely competitive today, especially because extreme innovator technologies are evolving how humans communicate and interact.

Extreme innovator businesses will all use some form of a business model that combines physical technologies with social technology and social organization. Physical technologies need to be socially designed so that people can use them as seamlessly as possible. The sweet spot is found at the intersection of physical technology and social technologies and organization. This sweet spot is the evolutionary launch pad for innovation.

Thus, as Beehacker further notes, extreme innovator companies must connect physical technologies with all the various social processes and interactions internally and externally to maximize efficiency effectiveness, diversity of opinions, ideations, and values.[6] This means that those who design extreme innovator companies must craft their innovation strategy and human interactions using the three superpowers of super intelligence, super speed, and super synergy.

Competition for Cooperation: The New Ecosystems

But how can evolution and the combining of the three superpowers co-exist when the most effective implementation of these superpowers calls for cooperation and collaboration to co-exist? Isn't evolution about survival of the fittest and purely individual, selfish interests? Not exactly. To win in today's market, alliances, partnerships, and ecosystems must join with diverse members to create extreme innovation in a collaborative effort. Intelligent cooperation is more likely to produce winners (survivors) than cutthroat competition that limits innovation possibilities. More minds working creatively towards a common goal are more likely to produce extraordinary results than fewer minds fighting with each other in narrowly focused competition.

Silicon Valley knows how to blitz scale and amplify companies to become extreme innovators, because it knows how to apply super intelligence. They often know who can do what, when, and where, as well as understand how to add the right relationships and resources to maximize growth through super speed and super synergy. In addition to its great accumulation of wealth, the Silicon Valley network and ecosystem has continued to have a successful built-in extreme innovator creation system.

For companies to emulate this system, they can audit their internal and external resources and connections to see what processes they have that match up to the Silicon Valley innovator process. But this will only succeed when paired with a similar type of Silicon Valley innovator mindset infused throughout the company.

How this can be created is the next question.

Scientists and Artists Create the Culture

Even though we are talking about innovation at lightning speed with data-driven physical and social technologies, you will always need the artist.

Steve Jobs saw in prior innovation at Xerox and with the Sony Walkman new future possibilities in the Mac and the iPod. He combined the vision of both the scientist and the artist, and we need to respect each domain and understand how they interconnect. In fact, biographer Walter Isaacson states about Steve Jobs that "his whole life is a combination of mystical enlightenment thinking with hardcore rational thought".[7]

In *The Eternal Law: Ancient Greek Philosophy, Modern Physics, and Ultimate Reality*, philosopher John H Spencer even shows how Jobs held fundamental ideas that align with Plato and what is more broadly known as the perennial philosophy. Jobs may have been a rarity, but we all can aspire to our own way of bringing together our inner scientist and artist. At the very least, we should be fostering an environment for others to do so. Our business will reap the benefits.

Silicon Valley understands that true extreme innovation is in the artistic design above the physical products and social processes. It's the elusive chemistry—the secret sauce—that makes someone an extreme innovator. No one knows for sure who will be the ultimate winners—sometimes referred to as the unicorns—but the extreme innovator approach that I am laying out here gives better odds for you to win and grow exponentially.

Explorers Ask Questions and Innovate

How does Neo in *The Matrix* solve problems and innovate to outdo the villain? By asking questions, which is at the heart of the explorer who is trying to innovate.

Q & A is at the core of extreme innovator businesses, processes, and products. The *Superpower Assessment Tool* in Chapter 15 was created by Q & A. It mirrors what drives innovators, and its simple but powerful search or query box Q & A aligns with the way we think and learn. AI works this way too, and other extreme innovator companies all utilize some type of Q & A language and communication. It's a growth business worldwide, representing more than $3 trillion a year and growing continuously.

For every question, there is an answer, but usually it's an answer that drives more questions. And the right questions are sometimes even more important than the right answers.

AI is the core technology that is driving extreme innovation, since it involves machines learning from other machines. This learning process enables us to have tasks done for us by voice commands, robots to serve us and do dangerous tasks, and augmented and virtual reality, which both change how we interact with the world, such as in the realms of surgery or mental health.

We can also add 3D printing to this list, as well as genetics. There is much, much more coming from extreme innovator companies to make the world more predictable and make it easier to get things done more quickly and inexpensively.

It's a Brave New World

Extreme innovation can use the three superpowers—super intelligence, super speed, and super synergy—to transform the world for the better.

There are so many new possibilities. It's time to jump into this brave new world.

It doesn't have to be a dystopia; we can make an amazing future together. But we do have to be brave, like a superhero, to do what it takes to become an extreme innovator.

Master the three superpowers to create an extreme innovator company and culture, and your world will be forever exciting and meaningful, and you will be able to help people make better decisions and live fuller lives.

And remember: machines can't be human, and it takes humans to process the results of data and connect the dots, much like Steve Jobs did. Step by step the artist evolves, and your business evolves also.

Extreme innovation means there is always more to learn and innovate. Let's go!

CHAPTER 2
Shhhhh! Secrets from the Bay Area

The innovation process moves forward based on the principle that the whole is greater than the sum of its parts. It works when it is executed successfully and communicated in a way that is intuitive and fully celebrates the magic of the initial concept. It watches for those lily pad moments in time and tech.

Innovation is the creation and application of a new idea or solution. David Bukus, best-selling author of *The Myths of Creativity: The Truth About How Innovative Companies and People Generate Great Ideas*, adds that creativity—the ability to generate novel and useful ideas—is the seed of innovation, but unless it's applied and scaled, it's still just an idea.[8]

Jeremiah Owyang, CEO of Crowd Companies, who completed a research report on the topic, surprisingly found that many innovation executives struggled to define what they do. The successful defined their programs as follows: "Innovation is the process of doing something new, that meets customers' needs."[9] So innovation can't just be about doing something new—it also must meet customers' needs. For example, MasterCard greenlights innovation programs that they anticipate will generate $1B in revenues from their partners and customers.

What makes Silicon Valley different?

Silicon Valley is a unique ecosystem that dates back 40 years. Innovation is the lifeblood there, propelled by a culture of risk-taking, a strong talent pool, and the right technology. The most extreme innovative companies have the following three things in common:

1. Innovation strategy that reinforces business strategy
2. Focus on diverse types of innovation
3. Three-pronged approach that requires new superpowers

Innovation Strategy that Reinforces a Business Strategy

Unfortunately, according to Booz & Company, only 20% of all global enterprises build and reinforce their business strategy with an innovation strategy. However, in Silicon Valley, they report that the number is 90%.[10] With innovation being the growth accelerator, the battle is for innovation.

Innovative ideas can be big or small, but breakthrough or disruptive innovation is something that either creates a new category or changes an existing one dramatically, rendering the existing market leader obsolete. I have built several new categories in my career. A new category accelerates success. We can disrupt ourselves or someone else can. To qualify as an innovation, a product either creates a new market or radically changes an existing one.

What is an innovation strategy?

An innovation strategy is a company's plan for ensuring that their business strategy is meeting the needs of clients today and in the future. It is a key factor in the success of companies, especially in a fiercely competitive environment.

Typical elements of an innovative strategy are:
- Vision and Inspiration
- Breakthrough Roadmap
- Evolving
- Ecosystems
- Being Inclusive
- Portfolio View
- Role Models
- Timeline for Each Type of Innovation
- Key Performance Indicators

Do you have one?

An innovative company has innovation embedded in its DNA structure or business model. For instance, Netflix itself is a disruptive innovation. The Netflix team has embedded innovation into its DNA, and therefore doesn't believe it needs a strategy to make innovation happen. However, most successful innovation companies have an innovation strategy that supports their business strategy.

<u>Silicon Valley is unique: most companies have well-defined strategic plans for innovation.</u>

Chapter 2

Focus on Diverse Types of Innovation

Most companies around the world tend to hone in on product innovation. Silicon Valley companies broaden their view and consider the elements of innovation beyond products. These C-suite executives tend to consider something far more important: *business model innovation and customer experience innovation* is as important as product innovation. For example, AirBnb has aligned culture, behavior, and operations around their customer experience, becoming one of the new stalwarts of experience building. Having strangers stay in people's homes has the potential for some challenges, but AirBnb focuses on the experience in three stages: before, during, after. They rank and rate for true two-way discussions to constantly make the experience the strongest possible. Their whole business model is about the new sharing economy.

Jeremiah Oywang's recently-published groundbreaking study on innovation found that product teams thought that product iteration was the primary form of innovation—but that is not sufficient when technology startups can quickly disrupt the game in just a few short years. He broke down the other types of innovations that impact clients:

1. Product Innovation
2. Business Model Innovation
3. Operational Innovation
4. Customer Experience Innovation

In the study, they found that the most sophisticated corporations deploy all four, and don't rely just on product iteration.[11]

CORPORATE INNOVATION IMPACTS
CUSTOMERS IN FOUR WAYS

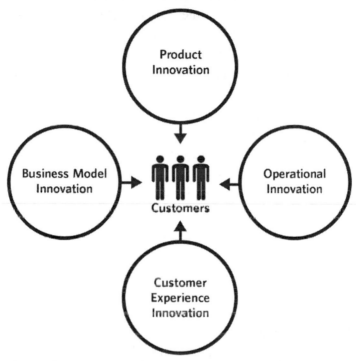

(Revised image used with permission from Crowd Companies)

Most executives consider innovation to be improving upon products or services. When a VP of Innovation or a Director of Research and Development is asked about innovation, they typically discuss product innovation.

But there is more covered by the term innovation than just product innovation. Not understanding the true definition of extreme innovation results in businesses getting destroyed by competition who embrace all elements.

Business model innovation is creating a new way of doing business. Think about Uber or Lyft: the service or product is the same, but the business model is different. For companies, this is typically a hard area to disrupt, as those currently in the business think that their current business model will continue to work well and don't consider the impact of new technology and ecosystems on their business model assumptions. Usually, companies don't consider this area until they see someone else trying to disrupt them, and by then it can be too late. Consider the brick and mortar retailers who have not anticipated the impact of Amazon and other e-commerce retailers.

Operational innovation involves improving the efficiencies of businesses, such as using robots for traditional factory jobs around the world.

And finally, there is customer experience innovation. This involves exploring how a customer views the end-to-end journey with the company. For example, Medallia, a San Francisco startup, focuses on helping companies create real-time dashboards to chart their overall client experience.

There are now Client Experience (CX) awards. Barclaycard won a CX award by focusing on critical components of organizational design for use in best practice experiences. The CX team created a governance model centered on key customer journeys, and assigned owners who have end-to-end accountability. The teams are empowered to make decisions for their journeys, including resource allocations.

Murat Uenlue, leader of Aircraft Delivery for Quantas Airlines, describes these innovation tactics as being like

LEGO pieces; the more pieces you have (i.e. the more you know), the better ideas you will be able to create.[12] Or perhaps it is best to see them as ingredients in a recipe; the more ingredients you have, the more refined dishes you can create. Executives who cannot apply multiple innovation tactics to their businesses will generally dish up the same tired ideas again and again.

Silicon Valley views innovation differently than the rest of the world

A Three-Pronged Approach that Requires New Superpowers

Silicon Valley approaches innovation with laser focus, closely integrating and focusing on:

- New Technology
- The Ecosystem
- Drawing on the Valley's Agile, Unique Culture

New Technology: The San Francisco Bay Area is the nation's most prolific source of new jobs in technology, according to the New York Times.[13] It is known for its deep technology and ecosystem, and the impact these forces have globally.

I lived in New York for a decade and loved the diversity of industries there. On every corner, there is a great designer or digital agency or even food entrepreneur. But in the Bay Area, tech is truly king. The diversity of tech (AI, Internet of Things [IoT], mobile, etc.) is vast and deep, and given that many of its workers are from outside of the United States, this means that there is huge diversity of thought as well.

The key to innovation is curiosity, and this technical expertise helps to ask and answer the next set of questions: How can we use artificial intelligence, Blockchain, and other technologies to make humans not only work together better, but also live more fulfilling lives?

Focus on the Ecosystem: There are so many startups around the world. It is easy to start a company, but to grow and scale it is another matter, and the Bay Area understands this phenomenon.

I once had a chance to listen in on a class led by Reid Hoffman, the founder of LinkedIn. It was about scaling companies at lightning speed, and Hoffman's view is that the Bay Area wins because it knows how to "blitz scale." Starting is not enough; you must be able to scale and grow. One of the key elements needed to scale is the ecosystem. This ecosystem is broad and wide. It consists of universities, influencers, collaborations of partners, and more. The attentive care and feeding of the ecosystem that happens in the Bay Area is unique to this place.

Drawing on the Valley's Agile, Unique Culture: Everyone talks about the unique culture in the Bay Area, but until you live here it's very difficult to really understand it. Accenture did a study on the culture by doing research on approximately 600 professionals, about half in the Bay Area and the other half throughout the United States. The conclusion: the Bay Area may be laid back, but its talent pool is ready for massive action when needed. Workers are committed but independent at the same time, and 71% are loyal to their employers.[14]

Silicon Valley is different in the types of work it offers and in the way its people think. The talent pool is competitive but cooperative. In general, they are extrinsically motivated, and intrinsically fulfilled. This culture can be created elsewhere, of course, but it requires focus and attention on many levels: deliberate government policies, universities that foster the best talent (especially in engineering), and companies embracing and collaborating with each other.[15]

Jeremiah Oywang
CEO, Crowd Companies

In the research on the Corporate Innovation Imperative, Crowd Companies CEO Jeremiah Owyang found that the biggest hindrance to an innovation program wasn't technology—it was resistance from the internal culture. In a survey of Fortune 1000 companies, 56% of respondents said they were struggling to foster a culture that would accept new programs that could seemingly cannibalize the primary revenue streams of the company.[16]

The study also found that companies had deployed up to 10 types of innovation programs—such as intrapreneur programs, centers of excellence, innovation outposts, excursions, tours, funding, and acquisition—all with varying degrees of sophistication. The most common among these was dedicated teams, and the least common was open innovation programs, where outsiders could contribute to the future programs.

The most advanced companies, like WL Gore, had deployed a common innovation methodology across all business units. Others, like MasterCard, had a dedicated budget set aside from the CEO which couldn't be withered, even during weakened company performance. Verizon's innovation teams even have internal teams that are focused on helping startups they've invested in to connect to existing business units, bridging multiple ways to partner.

[Thanks Jeremiah for your expert advice.]

That's the CliffsNotes version. Now what?

Careful study has heeded insights, but what else is needed?

- Super intelligence gained from new technology
- Super speed building an agile culture and processes
- Super synergy by focusing on the broader ecosystem

We will be diving into each of these superpowers to help generate extreme innovation!

Summary of the situation:

1. We are engaged in a war for innovation—extreme innovation for growth.
2. The greater Bay Area does this best at the moment, but there are no guarantees that they will continue to dominate.
3. The first difference is in developing and using an innovation strategy to enforce the business strategy.
4. The second difference is in their broad definition of innovation value for their clients.

5. And finally, their three-pronged approach to innovation built on new technology, ecosystems, and an agile culture.

6. To replicate this extreme innovation, three new superpowers are required:
   - i. Super intelligence
   - ii. Super speed
   - iii. Super synergy

Will you become one of the next leading innovators? The insights gleaned from the experts in this book will show you approaches and lessons that can help you before you jump in!

CHAPTER 3
The New Superpowers

Now you know that extreme innovation is about innovating with intelligence, speed, and synergy—all at the same time. But not just ordinary intelligence, ordinary speed, or ordinary synergy.

Extreme innovation demands extraordinary abilities: super intelligence, super speed, and super synergy. This chapter provides a basic overview of these superpowers. The next few chapters dive deeper into best practices and approaches.

NEW SUPERPOWERS FOR EXTREME INNOVATION

SUPER INTELLIGENCE	SUPER SPEED	SUPER SYNERGY
Leverage New Technology	Create Agility	Build Ecosystems
- Data Driven CEO	- Chief Cultural Strategist	- Chief Ecosystem Officer
- Ambidextrous CMO	- Guru of Cognitive Diversity	- Chief Connector & Empathy Officer
- Digital Prophet	- Chief Agility Officer	- Chief Obsession Officier

Many have tried to copy distinctive characteristics of Bay Area companies and culture. Most of them don't succeed, because they fail to adapt the "take away" to their home company or corporate culture. To create a similar culture, the key is to adapt what you learn to your own environment.

The next few chapters will articulate what types of characteristics are needed to bring back to your company to embrace innovation.

First, define your *current* powers. Dig into *each* of them. Why are these current powers insufficient or obsolete?

Next, explore with me the new superpowers. How do they differ from what you are currently doing? How will you develop and deploy them—alone and in combination?

The secrets in this book will result in different actions being taken by each reader, depending on how you need to adapt each of the superpowers.

As a reminder, **extreme innovation is combining new superpowers of intelligence, speed, and synergy to recognize, create, and jump on these new changes — the lily pads — with lightning speed.**

New Superpowers Overview:
- Super intelligence
- Super speed
- Super synergy

INNOVATION	EXTREME INNOVATION
- An innovation team drives and organizes	- Everyone innovates with super intelligence, speed and synergy
INTELLIGENCE	**SUPER INTELLIGENCE**
- Curious	- Cutting-edge explorers
- Data team	- Data hungry
- Some use of tech to innovate	- Organization infiltrated with tech savvy users
SPEED	**SUPER SPEED**
- Processes for incremental innovation	- Agile processes for Blue Sky Innovation
- Comfortable teams	- Cognitive Diverse teams
- Corporate culture – defined values, mission	- Co-created culture
SYNERGY	**SUPER SYNERGY**
- Alliances and partnerships	- Unusual partnering for win-win ecosystems
- Customer focused	- Customer obsessed
- Teams focused on customers	- Connected teams across customer success

Super Intelligence:

In superhero land, one of the top weapons wielded against the forces of evil is intelligence. In fact, in many scenarios, outsmarting the enemy is more valuable than outpunching them. In the same way, superheroes, companies, and countries need to take their intelligence to the next level.

41

Peter Parker was bitten by a spider to become Spiderman, but he used his technological knowledge to build his web-shooters!

Super intelligence is leveraging technology to provide your company with extraordinary insight. Given the extraordinary technology that already exists today, and new technologies that will exist in the future, some say that intelligence will be more valuable than speed in this next era.

Super intelligence will differentiate companies in the level of data use and the collection points of data, such as IoT, social media, and more. Data is coming in at an unprecedented speed. How companies use that data can help them craft their innovation strategy, innovate with all four types of innovation, and move with and ahead of their clients.

You need to explore what is required for your unique situation. As you look to deploy AI, Blockchain, and other technologies, you can disrupt companies and economies.

This change to super intelligence will also require new roles and characteristics, like CMOs who are skilled in technology and marketing, and CEOs who are data driven. Roles like Digital Prophets who will leverage the data for the innovation strategy will also be required.

We've always needed to be curious; now we must be cutting-edge explorers using technology to assist us.

Super Speed:

The Flash is probably the best known superhero for speed. He runs at the speed of light and uses his speed in surprising ways.

But if you think about the implications of super speed, there are other changes that are required in your reflexes, reaction times, and your overall body structure. For example, your skeletal structure and feet must be able to withstand more force.[17]

Super speed also requires superfast reflexes and brain power to comprehend what is happening (super intelligence). A perceptual shift is needed as you move at this new super speed, and that requires super-fast reactions to obstacles, much faster than an average person moving at a slower pace.

For super speed, what is required is the right infrastructure, a way to react faster, and quicker reflex times to respond to business changes. Infrastructure has driven changes in business practices on the ground: open offices, design centers, and even ways you can do your dry cleaning on campus to make work as frictionless as possible. Agile processes help customers and employees move at lightning rates toward innovation.

Innovation can benefit from agile processes, tools, and governance. Many companies have processes for incremental innovation, but not the extreme innovation required today. Companies develop processes because they have dedicated resources to their current sweet spot—their "bread and butter"—and extreme innovation (in this case, sometimes called "radical innovation") is risky and disruptive from a resource, capital, and management perspective.

Add to this mix a culture that is unique and supporting, and you can get things done at lightning speed.

Cognitive diversity is also critical. Working in teams that all look and sound alike may be comfortable, but it is not the best way to achieve blue sky innovation.

Consider these facts.

- **2009:** There was research highlighted in an *American Sociological Review* article with 500+ companies that found higher revenue, more clients, and bigger profits came from more cognitively diverse teams in terms of race and gender.[18]

- **2011:** Research highlighted in *The Product Innovation Journal* on management teams showed that diversity in education backgrounds and work histories produced more innovation for companies.[19]

- **2016:** Research highlighted in *Science Direct* was done with 20,000 companies across the world which discovered that more female executives drove more profit.[20]

The combination of different backgrounds, genders, races, and thought processes accelerates the innovation process.

Moving from ordinary speed to super speed will also require new roles and characteristics, such as having Chief Culture Strategists to ensure the company's culture moves along with the stage and the industry. With the importance of diversity of thought in teams, a Guardian of Cognitive Diversity will also be needed—and of course, with the focus on just pure speed, a Chief Agility Officer.

We've always needed to be fast; now we need to move at lightning speed in culture, infrastructure, and cognitive diversity.

Super Synergy:

In today's movies and TV shows, you can see superheroes coming together: *The Avengers, Supergirl, The Flash,* and more. We are drawn toward heroes who can "overcome any kind of unforeseen obstacle".[21] And there is also some unlikely partnering. Consider *Guardians of the Galaxy,* where a group of misfit superheroes partner to save the galaxy.

Super synergy is about finding ways to create a win-win-win scenario. It is about being client obsessed by including your customers in how you innovate, and putting yourself in their shoes. Did you know that less than 30% of an executive's time in a large corporation is spent with clients? In startups, it is 70%.[22] Combine that with working diligently with a larger ecosystem, and creating internal sizzle or passion, and innovation comes to the party.

The focus from synergy to super synergy requires some thought behind the roles. A Chief Ecosystem Officer would enable focus on a win-win-win with unlikely partners. A Chief Epiphany Guru would help get up the internal sizzle. With the importance of client obsession, a Chief Amazement Officer or Ambassador of Obsession would do the trick.

We've always needed to partner, but now we must move out of our comfort zones on alliances, and move into untraditional teams to propel us forward.

Super Intelligence: Cutting Edge Explorer

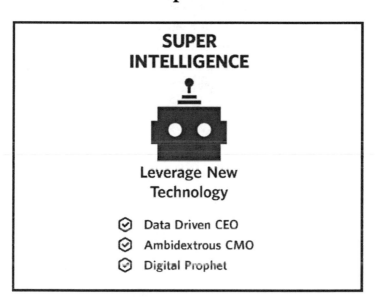

SUPER INTELLIGENCE

Leverage New Technology

- ⊘ Data Driven CEO
- ⊘ Ambidextrous CMO
- ⊘ Digital Prophet

If you remember back to our lily pad example, technology is a force that sometimes sneaks up on companies. Changes are growing exponentially. Silicon Valley is exceptionally great at creating new technology trends and then using that technology to drive innovation in operations, business models, and customer experience.

To survive and thrive in today's business world, companies need to encourage and enable extreme innovation, and that requires the three new superpowers. Whether or not you consider your company to be a tech company, the reality is that most (or all) companies are tech companies to one degree or another, because they all rely on technology.

In this chapter, we will look in more detail at how organizations are leveraging technology for extraordinary gains, propelling them to super intelligence:

1. Fostering growth of cutting-edge explorers
2. Data Hungry Organizations (ensuring the organization is armed with the correct data and intelligence tools)
3. Tech Savvy Users (use of technology to innovate—for example, using AI and virtual reality)

Elevator Pitch: Fostering Growth of Cutting-Edge Explorers

Cutting-edge explorers consist of teams that:
- ✓ ask lots of questions
- ✓ cultivate collaborative networking to share and learn from many diverse sources
- ✓ expand their presence and experiment

I grew up in North Carolina and always went to Wrightsville Beach in the summer. The Wright Brothers invented and flew the first plane. How did two brothers accomplish this feat? Well, many factors were involved, but they included studying how birds fly, critically reflecting on their own assumptions, asking a lot of questions, experimenting, persevering after setbacks, and gathering a lot of new data.

Most great innovations start with questions. Cutting-edge exploration begins with questioning everything. In

Amy Wilkinson's book, *The Creator's Code*, she interviews Elon Musk, who reveals that he always asked questions beginning from a very early age. Organizations that question the basics and the complexities are more likely to create disruptive innovation.

Questioning ideas and strategies is essential for an innovative organization. When we are children, we tend to question everything. In fact, according to online retailer Littlewoods.com, mothers are asked the most questions daily. Their report showed that "girls aged four are the most curious, asking an incredible 390 questions per day - averaging a question every 1 minute 56 seconds of their waking day." Their research indicates that the most successful entrepreneurs do not lose this questioning desire, and view it as crucial in helping them create the next big idea[23]

Companies that make it safe for their workers to innovate are the companies that win. Innovation is not about finding the perfect idea. Innovation is about questioning and iterating until you transform an idea into a profitable and scalable business model.

For example, in meetings each employee brings in one new idea. The idea challenges the status quo. Another good practice is for companies to bring in someone from outside the company to collaborate with teams, because they have a fresh perspective and aren't worried about disagreeing with the normal group.

Most boundaries are convenient fiction!

Don't let the highest ranking person's opinion shape your idea. Sometimes the best ideas come from outside the company or from those on the ground.

Chapter 4

Innovation Outposts and/or Centers:

Cutting-edge explorers also go out and learn. They may show up at their own store, or do an undercover assignment to learn what is happening. According to a recent white paper from Capgemini and Altimeter titled "The Innovation Game," 38% of the world's top 200 companies have set up innovation outposts or centers.[24]

Many companies end up setting up innovation labs in the Bay Area, where a creative spirit prevails. These innovation centers are prevalent in all industries, but manufacturing, telecom, automotive, consumer and retail products, and financial services are at the top of the chart.

For example, Swissnex, a network of innovation hubs sponsored by the Swiss government, is a great example of this phenomenon. I visited the facility in San Francisco and saw how Swiss companies in private-public partnership were taking advantage of this ability to broaden their scope of who they learn from. They have nodes in the world's most innovative hubs, connecting and facilitating a global network of diverse participants, from scientists to policy makers.

Another good example is Sephora, which opened an Innovation Lab as a giant real-world think tank at the port in San Francisco. The lab was designed to test new technologies that the retailer will then implement in its stores, online, and within its app. I had the pleasure of visiting the lab where the team "can ideate, test, dream, experiment and learn."[25] The goal is to bring in startups and experiment, learn, and create with others, as well as to explore how consumers will shop and consume products five years in the future. I also absolutely love their "Idea Central," which is a programmatic way that they crowdsource ideas from all their employees.

Creating innovation outposts and centers is a pragmatic and proactive way that explorers get their creative juices flowing. These centers enable outside learning, reward questions, and help teams to swiftly experiment and test.

Crowd Companies CEO Jeremiah Owyang has identified 10 types of innovation programs in the market today, such as a dedicated innovation teams and innovation tours.[26]

10 TYPES OF CORPORATE INNOVATION PROGRAMS

1	Dedicated Innovation Team
2	Innovation Center of Excellence (CoE)
3	Intrapreneur Program
4	Open Innovation (Hackathon or Internal Incubator)
5	Innovation Excursions
6	Innovation Outpost
7	Technology Education / University Partnership
8	External Accelerator Partnership
9	Startup Investment
10	Startup Acquisition

(Revised image used with permission from Crowd Companies)

Each of these programs has its positives and gaps when bringing extreme ideas into a corporation. And no corporation is doing all of these programs, so you can select the ones that are best for your culture and your goals.

For example, a partnership with an external accelerator can provide you early access to ideas and startups. My colleague runs RocketSpace, and they are partnering with corporations and startups in San Francisco. They began by betting big on a small startup at the time called Uber. Picking the right accelerator based on industry or technology focus will be a key essential mandate.

Executing on an Intraprenuer Program may be a way to initiate extreme innovation for your company. One of MasterCard's innovation programs, Launch Pad, is a one-week sprint to take ideas to fruition.

These are just some samples of ways of facilitating and developing extreme innovation. What ways can your organization do something similar, or perhaps take a whole new approach? Get innovative in how you foster innovation!

Key Terms:

- **Bootcamp**: Without any prior programming experience, basically anyone can enter these intensive on-the-job training programs, where in a matter of months you are spit out as a full stack software engineer with somewhere around a 95% hire rate. These bootcamps are in many ways a replacement for Computer Science degrees.
- **Dedicated Innovation Team**: A team inside of your corporation whose mission is to bring best practices inside the corporation.
- **Design and Innovation Jams**: A way to get a group of employees, clients, and other influencers to brainstorm together. It could be in person or online, and the goal is to take all the ideas—and these ideas

may be considered crazy ones—and figure out a way to sort through them to uncover the best ones.

- **External Accelerator Partnership**: Accelerators speed up the work done on startups and projects. If working with startups, they typically assist for a short amount of time—usually 90 days to six months. They offer mentors, education, and sometimes capital. Partnering with an external accelerator provides access to the best of the best startups and their extreme innovations.

- **Hackathon**: Typically a 24-hour engineering competition in which teams compete to create the best app from scratch. There may be specific challenges and technologies required, depending on the competition. Often prizes are awarded, even big money at the more prestigious events.

- **Incubator**: A program for businesses in the startup phase with the goal of promoting rapid growth by providing resources, networking, and support for the new company.

- **Innovation Excursion**: Excursions, or sometimes called custom immersion tours, begin with a group of executives or innovation members making a trip of a few weeks or months to innovation hubs like Silicon Valley. These trips serve to educate and help executives experience other cultures and innovation techniques.

- **Innovation Outpost or Lab**: These outposts and centers are physical spaces and/or teams set up by organizations in a global hub, and are usually associated with a technology center. The goal of the center or outpost is to leverage the super intelligence of the entire ecosystem of the area, including startups, industry, and academic ecosystems. These focused centers can accelerate innovation by discovering new tech or waves of disruption, and explore how to take advantage of it in context. Most of these centers want to test business models, technologies, operational excellence, and more. They are about disruption, not incremental changes.

- **Innovation Center of Excellence**: Its goal is to gather and create best practices, as well as create metrics, processes, and a culture that spurs innovation inside a larger company.

- **Intrapreneur Program**: This brings the best practices of entrepreneurs into the four walls of a corporation.

- **MVP – Minimum Viable Product**: Producing only what is required to test a new idea or concept.

- **University Partnership**: Many universities are partnering with corporations on innovation programs and classes to spur on innovation in different ways. I teach at Carnegie Mellon SV and their partnerships are vast and wide, with a number of corporations wanting to invest in their employees and programs.

And if the above ways of extreme innovation don't seem to be fitting, there are so many new innovation techniques to try.

- **Bodystorming**: This is a new technique to enhance brainstorming. It engages the whole experience—all body in—by having participants create a real experience with all the items that you would need when the idea goes live, but testing out in a real environment. Bodystorming enables empathy with the customers. In addition, you can see "why" it would work, and many challenges that may come up.

- **Painstorming**: This technique focuses on the customer's pain. Start by asking what pains, activities, needs, and new insights that have come up in the market.

- **Gamestorming**: This technique uses games to prod innovative thoughts and ideation.

- **The Long Table**: This is an ideation dinner party where the brainstorming is the first course.

- **The Business Model Canvas**: This model places the value of MBA training into a single page, and lots of startups in Silicon Valley use it to test business ideas quickly. (See image below.)

Extreme Innovation

Key Partners	Key Activities	Key Propositions	Key Relationships	Key Segments
	Key Resources		Channels	
Cost Structure			Revenue Streams	

⊚Strategyzer
strategyzer.com

(Revised image used with permission from Strategyzer.com)

Hackathons

Extreme innovator companies are leveraging crowds to come up with new disruptions as well. Hackathons are now becoming popular for many companies. A hackathon is a huge brainstorming session with execution of the ideas in programs, applications, or bots. Joshua Tauberer wrote a step-by-step guide based on running and participating in many hackathons, which I recommend.[27]

Personally, I find hackathons exciting. So many ideas are fresh and new.

At the ESPN and Girls in Tech Hackathon, ESPN acquired several new ideas from participant teams that they will experiment with at upcoming events.

At a hackathon, you see a great many extreme innovator characteristics. The participants present their ideas to a diverse room full of people. Sometimes ideas and teams come together or morph based on audience feedback. Usually over a weekend, the teams work with subject matter experts, continuously learning, to create their app or bot and then present it to the judges. In the ones I've attended, a lot of the participants have been to a bootcamp or coding school to learn the basics of coding before coming to the hackathon. The judges come in from companies, accelerators, and academia and may be venture capitalists or angel investors. After tons of drink and food, the winners are selected and the company that has sponsored the hackathon leaves with a plethora of great ideas. Many of these ideas are scooped up by incubators, and sometimes the teams form companies right on the spot in order to properly and legally protect their intellectual property grown from their new idea.

At SXSW 2017, Austin Mutschler, from Hack Arizona, discussed the value of Hackathons to companies as well. Hack Arizona is one the largest hackathons in the Southwest, where over 900 students and 25 sponsoring organizations come together for a weekend of agile software and hardware projects. This hackathon shapes students to be more creative, daring, and innovative. As more students enter the workforce, they will bring with them the skills gained from hackathons to the workplace. The Hack Arizona team teaches companies how to supercharge entry-level employees and create faster and more effective millennial teams.

Melissa Hargis
Co-Founder, Betagig

How a Hackathon Started a Company and Fostered Extreme Innovation

My co founder, Nicki Klein, and I turned a 48 hour hackathon project into a funded company in a matter of weeks. Eight months later, we now have our first paying client and a clear pathway to scaling our company quickly.

Elevator Pitch: How Did Our Innovation Occur?

Our innovation is Betagig, a way to *beta test* your next career. Students and job-seekers can use our job shadowing marketplace to try out careers before making a commitment. For example, you can see what it's actually like to work as a financial planner for a specific company by spending a day in the life observing one of their professionals. Likewise, companies can use Betagig to try out potential candidates and hire from the job shadowers that fit them well.

Just two and a half years ago, we were working in finance and education, not yet the full stack software engineers and budding entrepreneurs we are today. Now we are coding bootcamp grads, hackathon winners, self-taught mobile app developers, and newly funded female tech entrepreneurs. Surprisingly enough, we became all these things based purely on our overwhelming itch to make an innovative impact on our society, along with our super-speedy execution, and combined with what we've been joking about since we formed our dynamic duo: a grandiose sense of self that has given us the courage to walk into the fire over and over again and defy the odds.

Our secret sauce is that we are both technical. Can your new company scale as quickly without technical founders? It's tough to say, but it will certainly cost you some money and time, making it more challenging to get off the ground quickly.

Nicki and I do not come from a technical background, but we learned to code, and we did so without any prior programming experience and all in a matter of months. Attending a coding bootcamp was the beginning of our success.

I discovered these wondrous things called dev bootcamps, or coding bootcamps. Without having any prior programming experience, basically anyone can enter these intensive on-the-job training programs, where in a matter of months you are spit out as a full stack software engineer. Granted, you must be intelligent, highly motivated, and agile.

Meanwhile, Nicki was on a parallel path with zealous goals of starting a company and building the next great app. We met in the program and became fast friends, united by our innovative spirit and drive to succeed. We both shared the belief that learning to code would give us tremendous power. A couple of months after graduation, we were called upon by the founders of the bootcamp to participate in an upcoming hackathon.

A hackathon is typically a 24-hour engineering competition in which teams compete to create the best app from scratch all in a matter of days. Time is of the essence!

As a team of five women who were all very new coders, we shockingly took second place at the LA Techweek Hackathon. This sparked something important. Nicki finally could see clearly that her moment had come to start thinking about forming a company around an app she would build. And I, for the first time, realized that I already possessed everything it required to build an app that could truly be innovative. That sure happened fast! Just five months before we didn't even know how to code!

Now, I should take the time to enlighten you on one of our key strategies in our overall success and differentiation: standing out in the crowd. How do we accomplish this? Well, in the hackathon realm, this manifests in our wearing super feminine costumes. For us, it's all about using every-thing possible to our advantage. We are female engineers in a world of mostly men, so we choose to further stand out by defying stereotypes about women in tech. For this first hackathon in the tour, we dressed as cheerleaders.

Naturally, we showed up as the only two competitors in costume. Perfect! Exactly what we wanted. We built a mo-bile app in Swift, after only learning the language and plat-form just three weeks prior. We ending up winning $5,000. This was a great boost to our confidence. This was exactly what we needed to propel us into our next hackathon. Re-ally, it's all about whatever confidence you can muster up; real or artificial, it doesn't matter.

The next on the list was the Launch Hackathon in San Francisco. This one was huge. There would be 1,500 devel-opers of the top caliber, all competing for an investment in their not-yet-built app and entrance into the Launch Incu-bator. We just needed an unbeatable idea. It's crucial to show up at a hackathon with an idea in place. This is the beauty of a hackathon: it forces you to enter into think-tank mode on a very tight deadline. The hackathon was just one week away; we couldn't sit around for months waiting for an innovative idea to pop in our heads.

ᕼ betagig

(Revised image used with permission from Betagig)

We were forced to come up with a killer idea right then. I remember very clearly the day we conceived Betagig. We were walking down Haight Street. We saw all sorts of interesting individuals. "Nicki! Wouldn't it be great to have an app where you could experience a day in the life of someone else? I mean, look at all these fun people! I would love to see what it's like to step in someone else's life for a day." Nicki was on board but immediately had her own insight: "Yes! But for careers! You try out another person's job for a day!" Thus, Betagig was born. We sat in Golden Gate Park, brainstorming ideas for an app name. We made two lists: one of synonyms for *trying out* and another for *job*. And we arrived at Betagig: *a way to beta test your next career.*

The following weekend we rolled into the hackathon, heads held high, and sporting fifteenth century queen costumes, crown and all.

It was a 48-hour hackathon, meaning more time to build but also more time without sleep. In the end, this hackathon was perfectly executed. We made Top 40, then pitched to another round of judges. Then we made Top 20, then pitched again on stage. Then we made Top 5. We were finalists! This meant we would be pitching on the big stage the next weekend in front of all Launch Festival attendants.

We had five days to continue working on our app before we would take the final stage. We spent time obsessively trying to gain the advantage over our competitors. What was the best way to accomplish this? Well, we decided we would go out and get customers. We took advantage of the fact that numerous important companies were attending the Launch Festival that week. Some of the judges had expressed concerns regarding the ability to ever get companies on board to allow job shadowers in their offices. *What was in it for the company?* they wanted to know. So we frantically contacted any inside connects we had for intros, and for the rest we simply did a cold approach in person.

We ended up pitching on stage with nine companies wanting to use Betagig, including three huge companies that everyone knew. We won first place.

Winning the Launch Hackathon changed our lives. A few weeks later we received an initial investment in Betagig and entrance into the Launch Incubator. We were on our way to a fighting chance at success.

Months later, Nicki and I now have a growing company, with employees, our first paying client with many more in the pipeline, and a new large investment for a real chance at making this thing big.

Business leaders can begin their innovation by forming a founder team with at least one technical co-founder. If you're not technical, then become technical. Just having an idea does not get the job done. Ideas are a dime a dozen. If you are really serious about creating an innovation, you must be passionate enough about your idea to be willing to do everything possible (including gaining new skills!) to bring your product to life.

[Thanks Melissa for your expert advice.]

Let's Get This Party Started:

Here are some of the best ways to get started in making your organization become a cutting-edge explorer:

- Implement questioning sessions in planning meetings.
- Determine which of the 10 extreme innovation programs is right for your company or country.
- Do employee and customer jams using technology to uncover great ideas:
  - o Review other companies' best practices
  - o Explore the right technology to use
  - o Examine university help
- Set up an innovation hub or outpost. I would recommend a deep dive into the paper "The Innovation Game" by Capgemini and Altimeter.
  - o Items to consider are:
    - ▪ Is it a dedicated center or team?
    - ▪ How many centers and locations will there be?
    - ▪ Governance model
    - ▪ Funding mechanism
- Develop a hackathon strategy:
  - o Internal
  - o External with customers and partners

Chapter 4

o   Expansion plans with universities
o   Keep on asking questions and networking
    with people who are smarter than you

CHAPTER 5

Super Intelligence: Data Hunger Driven by IoT and Social Media

The previous chapter discussed fostering growth of cutting-edge explorers, and in this chapter on super intelligence, we'll look at the importance of being data hungry.

The mantra for an extreme innovator culture is: don't let opinions trump evidence.

Data Hungry Organizations

When an organization asks lots of questions and learns from a variety of sources while expanding their experimentation and presence, a lot of data is generated. This is the next characteristic of super intelligence: being hungry for that data!

Being data hungry is a trait of an extreme innovator. According to DataMation, there will be a trillion gigabytes of data by the end of 2017.[28] It is growing so fast that there may soon be no words to describe how much of it there is. But conquering big data is linked to extreme innovation.

In the Boston Consulting Group's (BCG's) new research, "The Most Innovative Companies 2016: Getting Past 'Not Invented Here'," data supporting the hungry trait is strong. BCG found that self-reported "strong innovator" companies are more than 4.5 times more likely to generate ideas from big data and analytics than their weak counterparts—and that 65% of strong innovators mine big data or social networks for ideas.

In that same BCG report, the data supports the claim that strong innovators have exceptional skills and insights on gathering data both inside and outside the organization. The report highlights "global patents, scientific literature, semantic networks, and venture funding databases." The use of data is found throughout the innovation process— from new ideas to the creation of the product or service and investment and go to market.

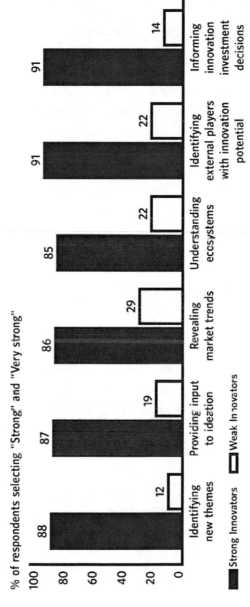

EXHIBIT 4 | Strong Innovators Use External Data Throughout the Innovation Process

HOW WOULD YOU RATE YOUR COMPANY'S SKILL AT LEVERAGING BIG DATA AND ADVANCED ANALYTICS TO HELP WITH EACH OF THE FOLLOWING ASPECTS OF INNOVATION?

% of respondents selecting "Strong" and "Very strong"

Identifying new themes: 88 / 12
Providing input to ideation: 87 / 19
Revealing market trends: 86 / 29
Understanding ecosystems: 85 / 22
Identifying external players with innovation potential: 91 / 22
Informing innovation investment decisions: 91 / 14

■ Strong Innovators □ Weak Innovators

Source: BCG Global Innovation Survey, 2016
Note: The "Strong innovator" and "Weak innovator" categories are based on survey responses.

(Revised image used with permission from BCG)

The data hungry DNA that is required to be an extreme innovator consists of:

- **Data collection** or mining both inside and outside your company
    - o Very simply, collecting the right data means that you need to understand the sources of the data that are required for insight.
    - o Collecting data today is a huge job. There are structured and unstructured data sources, as well as social and sensor based data (the biggest is Internet of Things, which is covered in our next section).
- **Data exploration**
    - o Data exploration leverages experimentation to discover questions and answers that might not have even been thought of to date. Statistics and modeling come into play in this stage. Data exploration makes heavy use of statistics to experiment and get answers to questions that managers might not have thought of previously.
- **Data cleansing**
    - o Data cleansing involves ensuring that the data is relevant and valid. I've had clients run to their boards with discoveries that were built on faulty data. As the saying goes, garbage in, garbage out.

- **Data analytics to discover insights**
    - Just having the data isn't good enough. The data need to be analyzed to determine insights that can result in business actions.
- **Sharing**
    - I know this seems obvious, but some companies gather and analyze the data, but never have a forum to share the data on a regular basis.

As shown in this graphic, data by itself is not valuable. It is when data becomes actionable knowledge and insight that it becomes a weapon. Some people compare data to oil: it is not valuable until you extract it!

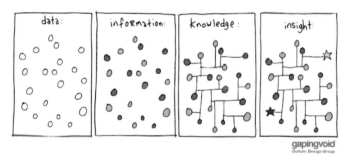

(Image used with permission from Gapingvoid)

Key Terms:

- **Big Data:** A collection of data from traditional and digital sources inside and outside your company that represents a source for ongoing discovery and analysis

- **Structured data:** Data that is in a text form and is easily organized by traditional databases.

- **Unstructured Data:** Non text based data like voice, video, or picture. An example might be a video on YouTube or even a tweet with an attached picture.

- **Data Lake:** A repository for raw, native data.

- **Data Scientist**: A skilled person who manages and drives data in a corporation. They interpret data, combine data sources, ensure consistency, create visualizations, and communicate insights from the data. It is one of the top skills needed today.

- **The 4 (or 5) V's:** Many companies use terminology to talk about data in the form of 4-5 words that begin with the letter V. So, give me a V and let's go through them!
    - o **Volume** is the amount of data
    - o **Velocity** is the speed of the data generation
    - o **Veracity** is the accuracy and reliability of the data
    - o **Variety** is the type of data
    - o **Value** is the worth or importance of the data

Show me the Money – Profit:

IDC, an analyst group, showcases that by 2020, "organizations able to analyze all relevant data and deliver actionable information will achieve an extra $430 billion in productivity benefits over their less analytically oriented peers."[29]

Big data is an extreme innovation accelerator.

Change the World – Purpose:

Big data is being used throughout the world for social good.

I was at the Consumer Electronics Show in 2017, and saw how SnapChat leveraged its power for good. A bit of background: according to Comscore, in year to year growth, Snapchat added 25-34 year users (103%) and 35+ users (84%) faster than 18-24 year old users (56%). Snapchat's own data claims 12% of its nearly 50 million daily users in the U.S. are 35 to 54.[30] Snapchat used its powerful data and identified influencers to run a CyberBully campaign called "I am a Witness."

How will you leverage your data for good?

Let's Get This Party Started:

1. Design a plan for a data-hungry initiative to change the culture to expect the use of data.
2. Hire a great team of data scientists. This area will only grow in its impact on innovation.
3. Learn and experiment.
4. Ensure all data sources are being used. Internet of things will be one of the biggest sources of data in the future, which we will cover in the next section.

> # It's not about **Big Data.**
> # It's about **Right Data.**

Brian Buntz
Content Director, Internet of Things
Institute, Penton

How Internet of Things Impacts Innovation

Elevator Pitch: What exactly is IoT?

When most people hear about the Internet of Things, they think of things like a connected refrigerator that sends snapshots from within your refrigerator to your smartphone. Or a smart thermostat that you can control from your phone. Or they think of some other kind of smart gadget.

But the fact is, the Internet of Things is much grander than that, and the security concerns surrounding the technology, though real, often don't portray the full story. In reality, the Internet of Things is poised to transform our world in several ways. Cars and trucks are beginning to drive themselves, as are tractors. Healthcare is in the process of getting much smarter, enabling doctors (and algorithms) to track patients remotely—whether they are located across the hospital or in a different country. And the manufacturing field has already begun to enter the next Industrial Revolution, or Industry 4.0.

But what is the Internet of Things, anyway? **It's basically a network of physical "things"— devices that are connected to a network.** In one sense, the IoT is the next stage of cloud computing. With the advent of cloud computing, companies across the world discovered that it helped them share resources and perform business processes more efficiently. It also gave consumers more flexibility and tools. Want to have a friend across the world help edit a text document in real time? No problem. Just share a Google doc. Want to listen to nearly any song imaginable on your phone in an airport? Just open up Spotify on your smartphone and stream it from Spotify's servers over your cell connection. That's cloud computing.

The Internet of Things, however, opens up a whole new realm of possibilities. It takes the concept of the Internet, which is used by billions of people every day for applications ranging from online banking to live-streaming video, and applies it in completely novel ways.

The Internet of Things will dwarf the Internet in several ways. Here is a case study that explores this.

Case Study: IoT Prodding Innovation in a Company

The IoT lets a tech-savvy farmer track what kinds of pests are invading his apple orchard from his living room.

A Canadian company known as Semios, for instance, is using IoT to help farmers monitor orchards and vineyards and then use pheromones to help fight pests, therebyhelping them cut their use of insecticides.

In Ammon, Idaho, for instance, the IoT helps keep students at Sandcreek Middle School safe. A network of connected cameras and a gunshot detection system in the school work together to monitor for a school shooting. In the event that a gun is fired in the school, the cameras focus on where the shots came from, taking footage of the shooter and relaying this information within seconds to the local police.

IoT could also help save the rainforests. The Amazon Basin Conservation Association, for instance, is using drones to help spot illegal logging and mining in Peru.

And the IoT enables the German industrial company Siemens to offer its trains as a service rather than a product. The Spanish rail company Renfe has signed a performance-based contract with Siemens that is based on its high-speed trains running on time. Siemens says that the trains that run from Barcelona to Madrid run on time 99.9% of the time. The model enables passengers to be reimbursed for delays of more than 15 minutes. Sensors on the train also enable predictive maintenance—anticipating when equipment failure will happen and performing maintenance to prevent problems from happening. Algorithms can predict when a potential failure might occur, enabling technicians to plan repairs while trains are in service, rather than in a service center. The trains can track billions of data points, factoring in data about the rails, the slope of the track, the weather, as well as the usual things like speed, mileage, and braking performance. 100 rail cars could generate 100 to 200 billion data points annually.

Why does all of this matter from a business perspective? In this case, it helps Renfe stay more competitive. In the past, nine out of 10 passengers traveling between Barcelona and Madrid took a plane. Now, half of these passengers opt to take the train.

In the automotive realm, GM has projected that it will gain $350 million of incremental profit in the next three years from connecting their cars.

The possibilities are so vast that GE is betting that the industrial internet—or the IoT in the industrial realm—will add $15 trillion to global GDP in the next 20 years.

[Thanks Brian for your expert advice.]

IoT is driving all four types of innovation

There are four types of innovation, and we see IoT's impact on all four by providing extra data from sensors.

Business Process: Based on new data that is gathered from sensors, business processes can not only iteratively be made better, but also can exponentially be changed. A fun and simple but powerful example is Command Propel. It is an IoT product for fishing that uses sensors to measure, weigh, and GPS tag where a fish was caught. It is being used in major fishing tournaments, changing the way data is collected to determine the winner. Imagine the new data that fishermen and the tournament now collects.

Product: IoT is impacting products, but we have only begun to see its impact on the world: from littleBits, a startup that is creating sensor oriented blocks to teach and train the next generation, to Hatch Baby, a San Francisco startup using senses to keep babies healthy. Urban 3D, a startup from Brazil, is even adding sensors to concrete to sense issues in foundations from the concrete out! All of these products are now providing big data to further analyze and enhance services and knowledge.

Operational: CarForce, a startup out of San Francisco and Dallas, connects cars back to the dealer when the customer is at a point of need for service using sensors. It adds value to customers, eliminating the way they track service today. For dealers, the solution provides them with new operational ways to service cars. This data alone increases the dealers' service, and increases the safety for the consumer.

Customer Experience: IoT is impacting B2B and B2C experiences. Entrepreneur Kate Stone created conductive ink to print IOT sensors that make playable paper posters. This poster can enable someone who touches it to play a song, or a greeting, making the poster interactive. This technique can be used in B2B training posters or B2C for selling concerts or albums. The data gathered from what people press on and use interactively is used to further innovate both designs and products.

For some sample vertical or industry based use cases, see the chart below.

Vertical	Sample IoT Application
Transportation	Usage-based car insurance

	Vehicle telematics
	Driving and parking assistance technology
	Self-driving cars
Smart Agriculture	Pest detection
	Smart irrigation
	Wireless soil / moisture monitoring
	Energy management / connected HVAC
	Smart lighting
	Security sensors
Smart Cities	Smart street lights
	Smart parking
	Gunshot detection systems
	Monitoring trash can levels
Utilities	Smart grid
	Tracking municipal drinking water / waste water
	Smart meters

	Sensors to track performance of solar power stations and wind farms
Manufacturing	Sensors on factory floor
	Predictive maintenance for equipment
	Product tracking
	Connected industrial controllers
	Smart robots
Healthcare	Connected medical devices
	Smart home sensors designed to help elderly "age in place"
Smart Homes	Connected thermostat
	Smart lighting
	Smart refrigerators
	Connected security cameras
	Wireless burglar alarms

(Graphic created in collaboration between Brian Buntz and Sandy Carter)

Let's Get This Party Started:

Once you begin to see the potential of digitizing the physical world, it is time to ask how it can help optimize your business, or how it can enable a new one.

- Before you launch an IoT project, though, you should first take a careful look at your biggest business challenges. Get together with your team and make a list of things that you know and don't know about your core business challenges. Then, study the capabilities of IoT technologies like connected sensors, edge computing, etc. and reflect on how they could help address your business challenges, and estimate where you will see the greatest ROI. Because of the immense potential, it is easy to be overwhelmed.

- The next step is to work together with your team to develop a step-by-step plan to get there and a clear sense of who the most important stakeholders are. The first step in your IoT should have a clear ROI attached to it. Ideally, it should be a small project that is a learning experience that gives you a frame for pursuing more ambitious goals. Many cities across the United States, for instance, are installing smart lighting because they can prove that it will save them money.

- Rinse and repeat. Once you have a model of success, repeat and learn, continuously getting better in order to pursue other IoT-inspired projects.

Perils:

Perhaps one of the biggest problems with the Internet of Things is the fact that few people have seen its potential to drive improved business outcomes. It's easy to add connectivity to devices, but it is tougher to do so in a way that makes sense. If a company makes toasters, will adding connectivity and computing power to the device give them a competitive advantage? Maybe not. But what if you are an airplane maker and the connectivity and computing power you are adding to the jet engines can help optimize fuel consumption? A commercial jet uses about 1 gallon of fuel per second—that's thousands or tens of thousands of gallons of fuel per flight. Even if you just saved 1% of fuel consumption, that would be about 360 gallons worth of fuel for a 10-hour flight.

Despite the significant potential of the Internet of Things, deploying the technology is by no means easy. There is a lack of interoperability or agreed-upon standards. Deploying an IoT solution also can require an unprecedented level of collaboration within your organization, and likely outside it as well. The IoT is forging alliances between marketers, mechanical engineers, coders, sensor makers, and security experts. Your company's culture needs to be able to accommodate collaboration between all of the above and more.

The other obvious problem is security. Many companies working on IoT projects rush to market with the hope that they can wow their customers. But it's worth taking the time to build in security from day one and to constantly address security throughout product development. If you aren't an expert in security, hire one or find a partner to work with.

Data poses another significant hurdle for many IoT applications. First of all, who has access to it isn't always clear. And it is easy to underestimate the volume of data that you are generating or the work it will take to make sense out of it. You should think carefully about what to do with your data. Should you send it to the cloud? Or can you process it locally at the edge? Or do you want a mix of both?

Promises:

20 years from now, those who wrote off the Internet of Things may have the same reputation as those who called the Internet a fad in the 1990s. IoT promises to digitize the physical world and, as a result, offers innovative companies a competitive advantage. It can enable companies to expand their product offerings with services—selling, for instance, trains as a service rather than a product.

The IoT promises to fundamentally change how we work and how we do business. Sensors in cars or in factories can prevent problems before they happen. Warehouses could begin to stock and replenish themselves.

For marketers, IoT can provide new ways of tracking the customer journey, and give companies the ability to forge new connections with customers. This could have far-reaching consequences for many industries. Consider the automotive field, for instance. 10 years ago, if a car maker heard from a driver, it was probably because the driver wanted to sue them because of a fault with the car. But connected cars give automakers a direct connection to drivers and passengers and even offer them new types of products. Tesla, for instance, uses driver behavior to improve the accuracy of their self-driving Autopilot feature, which might reduce crashes.

With IoT, the possibilities are nearly limitless. The question is: 10 years from now, will you say that you were disrupted by it? Or are you going to say that you tapped the power of this technology to disrupt your industry?

CHAPTER 6
Super Intelligence: Artificial Intelligence and Bots

Tech Savvy Users – Artificial Intelligence

Ray Kurzweil, chief of engineering at Google, has said that artificial intelligence (AI) will reach human levels in the next 12 years. While this may be an overestimation, by 2045, scientists are likely to be able to multiply the capabilities of this intelligence, catapulting the human biological machine intelligence of the world by a billion. Imagine the future.

AI's promise is unprecedented and staggering. Lufthansa is creating flying autonomous cars. Amazon has Alexa engaging in household assistance. Smaller startups such as suitX are helping those with labor intense roles work longer with their own "X-Men-like" suit. Recruiters are being screened for unconscious bias in their hiring processes.

Imagine the possibilities—and the potential peril. Will machines become smarter than us? Could they take over the world? Naysayers believe AI could divide the world into two camps: for and against, causing a global civil war. World-renowned cosmologist Steven Hawking warned that AI could end humanity. Elon Musk has said that AI is the world's greatest existential threat.

Both the hazards and the potential rewards are great. Within this framework, every business leader must understand its potential and value to the bottom line. It has enormous potential to strengthen a company's core mission.

Chapter 6

Elevator Pitch: What exactly is it?

Artificial Intelligence (AI) is simply leveraging software to simulate tasks and processes that humans do today. An AI system reasons according to a set of rules, and it gives the appearances of learning and understanding. I say "gives the appearances," because this claim about computers learning and understanding is controversial, but the arguments for and against from philosophers and scientists are not our concern here. What does matter for our purposes is that AI is extraordinarily powerful, and it will continue to grow in its power and impact on our lives in diverse ways. Businesses around the world are leveraging AI to strengthen their competitiveness, and our dependence on AI is going to grow.

AI can help you get the right information to the right person at the right time. It can automatically extract valuable insight from data and assist with decision support. AI can amplify productivity through task automation. Basic functions today include visualization, facial recognition, conversational direction, and converting text to speech and speech to text.

According to Gartner, by 2020, 85% of customer interactions will be managed without a human. The value of AI is that it enables businesses to be smarter in their interactions. 80% of executives believe artificial intelligence improves worker performance and creates jobs, as per Narrative Science.[31] AI depends on data and training. Machines are not naturally smart; you must spend time educating them, in ways not so different in some respects from the education of children.

Most large software companies have started to integrate machine learning into their platforms as an easy to start option. Salesforce and others have found interesting starting points, such as simple templates and kits for developers to get started. Given that over $1.5B in venture capital was invested in AI startups through June of 2016 (a 300% increase year to year),[32] there are many startups set up to disrupt this space and leverage industry knowledge to create solutions.

AI is a driver of extreme innovation. Ericsson Consumer Lab, in its annual trend report titled "The 10 Hot Consumer Trends for 2017 and beyond," said that 35% of advanced internet users want an AI advisor at work.

Bots are the hot new AI use case. What are they? Bots are software that has messenger capability, leverage AI, and respond in a human like way to text requests. Everyone from Vogue, to Dominos to Poncho – a weather bot- is getting in on the action.

"Consumer behavior has shifted from social networks to messaging platforms such as SMS, Facebook Messenger, Apple iMessage, Slack and WeChat. The growth of the four largest messaging apps exceeds that of the four largest social networks. A new marketing channel is an exciting opportunity to experiment with fresh ad formats and connect with consumers in novel ways. Businesses also enjoy less competition, less ad fatigue, and potentially exponential returns on marketing investment dollars (ROI)." Adelyn Zhou, CEO, TOPBOTS

Chapter 6

AI is driving all four types of innovation

There are four types of innovation and we can see AI's impact on all four.

Business Process: It can help in extreme innovation for step change improvements in how processes work. For example, consider Atipica, a talent discovery engine that uses human and artificial intelligence to help companies understand the lifetime of their recruiting data. Atipica is innovating the way that companies view unconscious bias. It can learn patterns in recruiting and hiring, and identify gaps and actions that need to be addressed in order to hire the very best team possible.

Product: Products are a hot spot for extreme innovation. AI can take products to the next level of functionality. For example, RayBaby is an IoT device that can track a baby's respiration and analyze the data. It utilizes ultrawideband radar technology, which works much like ultrasound, and using AI it learns when the movement is related to breathing or just normal movement. Another example is a Forbes Most Innovative Company, MasterCard. One of the reasons they selected MasterCard was for their new AI-based facial recognition for reducing friction in the payment area. They are experimenting with using selfies as a way to identity who you are before making a payment.

Operational: Operational excellence has extreme innovation potential, too. AI is great at finding the questions that you are not even asking, whether that is in predictive maintenance, or sales and marketing functions. For example, according to Inc. Magazine, 6sense, a startup based out of San Francisco, is helping companies like Cisco predict sales.

Customer Experience: The way that humans interface today is changing. Extreme innovation is occurring through chatbots powered by AI. Consider Avaamo, a startup that makes a suite of chatbots to change experiences in multiple industries—for instance, the way you buy your clothes online or the way you make your airline reservations. Unlike automated voices over the telephone, with chatbots, most people don't even realize they are not talking to a person.

Now let's take these innovation areas and show how AI's functions of automation, classification, and prediction can help extreme innovators. In a session with Rob May, he shared with me his Intelligent Framework that aids extreme innovators. Taking your business, brainstorm on how AI could assist your extreme innovation with customers, products, and operations.

For instance, this is an example of a framework that you might use:

	Customer Experience	Product	Operation	Business Model
Automate				
Classify				
Predict				

(Revised image used with permission from Rob May, Talla, modified by Sandy Carter with approval)

I have used this framework myself, and I have filled in some ideas below around areas that may work for your business:

	Customer Experience	Product	Operation	Business Model
Automate	E.g. Bots to provide customer Service from Tweets		E.g. Information gathering before meeting	
Classify	E.g. Highest value users for special services	E.g. Auto-create groups for sharing		E.g. Points of friction for improvement
Predict	E.g. Predict the most loyal clients based on initial usage	E.g. Pre-select new filters and tools a user might love	E.g. next step in employee training	E.g. Most valued new service

Extreme Innovation

(Revised image used with permission from Rob May, Talla, modified by Sandy Carter with approval)

This intelligent framework is just a way to begin the extreme innovation cycle with teams to discover new ways to differentiate with AI.

Key Terms:

a) **Bots.** Bots are growing in importance. They are messaging applications mostly with a conversational interface to simplify a complex task. The top three use cases today for bots are client service and support, personal assistants, productivity, and communications. "Messaging apps are the platforms of the future and bots will be how their users access all sorts of services," says Peter Rojas, Entrepreneur in Residence at Betaworks, an American startup studio and seed stage venture capital company based in New York City.

b) **Machine learning.** Machine learning is often confused with AI. AI is the broader concept. Machine learning is about a portion of AI that enables machines to take the data and learn for themselves.

c) **Corpus of Knowledge.** A corpus of knowledge is a collection of knowledge and data that is used to train an AI system. The old adage, "garbage in, garbage out" is true in any AI system. Directed inputs are critical. You need to build up the knowledge base of your AI system.

Show me the Money – Profit:

AI is essential for optimizing business processes. Customer service and maintenance are two of the first use cases that have shown profit optimization. Others include contract analysis and medical. On the revenue side, customer experience is one of the top use cases. For example, using personalization based on personality for selling, or trade off analysis for insurance claims and fraud detection.

AI Use Cases

Marketing Personalization	Facial / visual recognition
Contract analysis	Real time translation
Preventive maintenance	Price quotes
Trading optimization	Error prevention
Assisted Diagnosis	Crime fighting
Autonomous cars	Customer service
Selling optimization	Personal Assistant

Change the World – Purpose:

AI can help foster a company's core mission in a purpose-driven way. It can remove tedious work from employees and enable them to work on more insightful and interesting work. Many companies are leveraging AI to change the world for good.

For instance, companies are using AI to identify and help provide solutions to mitigate unconscious bias, or to identify better ways to help the underprivileged optimize their budgets. Next moves: how companies will leverage the technology for social good.

Let's Get This Party Started:

The best ways to get started with AI are the following:

- Educate your teams on the new AI kits and methods through learning systems like online courses, innovation team workshops, and coding classes.
- Explore use cases of those inside and outside your industry.
- Experiment and test use cases.
- Start small with personal assistance or internal communication personalization to learn the ins and outs.

CHAPTER 7

Super Intelligence with VR/AR as Innovation Accelerators

In the past 12 months, I have visited beaches in Chile and trekked up Mt Everest. Hanging from a chopper a couple thousand feet above the ground was also exciting. All of this, of course, happened through my Virtual Reality headset.

AR and VR's promise is unprecedented and staggering. Lowe's Innovation Labs has experimented in stores with VR to visualize your new kitchen; the Dallas Cowboys and Tampa Bay Rays are using AR/VR in training; Sephora now has an AR makeup artist; Virginia hospitals are using VR to treat PTSD; and TOMS leverages VR for a virtual giving trip experience where clients can see how a shoe to someone in a third world country is appreciated. Even luxury brands like Sotheby's have used VR to sell apartments before there was a brick on the property!

AR/VR has the potential to be an innovation engine. Everyone in your team—from marketing, to design, sales, customer service reps, and development—should experience the potential of this new technology to help in your innovation strategy. But be aware that virtual reality is finally coming out of the so-called trough of disillusionment which is inflated expectations that are sometimes not delivered on. There is still work being done on the technology—but don't be late here.

Chapter 7

Elevator Pitch: What exactly is it?

Virtual Reality (VR) immerses the user in a virtual world via a headset that largely isolates them from the real world. Augmented Reality (AR), on the other hand, inserts virtual objects and information into the real world, augmenting your experience via a headset that, ideally, is as discreet as possible.[33] VR and AR are very similar. They both desire to immerse the user in the environment, but they approach it differently. With VR, the environment is separate from the "real world" and is usually something that is totally unreal. In AR, while in touch with the "real world," interaction with virtual objects drives an augmentation of the environment.

More than nine million virtual reality headsets were shipped in 2016, per research by IDC.[34] Digi-Capital released a report that projected AR and VR would be a $150 billion market by 2020. Only $30 billion of that will be VR.[35]

The value of AR / VR is not just in gaming but also in marketing products, showcasing new designs, training and education, healthcare, architecture, manufacturing, retailing, transportation, logistics, exploration, and the military. According to the latest research from Tech Pro Research report, 48% of companies are considering adopting VR and 67% of companies are considering adopting AR.[36]

The three most popular areas where AR is used are simulation exercises, employee testing and training, and for use in products. Over $500 million in venture capital was invested in AR/VR startups in 2016, and Digi-Capital estimates it will be $120B by 2020.[37]

Key Terms:

a) **Augmented Reality (AR):** Augmented Reality or AR is defined as a "technology used to produce an enhanced environment" (per CrispIdea Research[38])

b) **Virtual Reality (VR):** Virtual Reality or VR is defined as "immersive, interactive experience generated by a computer".

c) **Mixed Reality (MR):** Mixed Reality is the combination of virtual plus the real world experience.

AR/VR is driving all four types of innovation

The four types of innovation that we discussed in Chapter 2 are all impacted by AR/VR:

1. **Business Process:** AR/VR changes the game in the way that your business processes are improved, but also in how they are extremely innovated. In the case study in this chapter, SmartVizx is an example of a complete change in business. Their solution changes the way the process of design and selling is done in the construction field. Imagine the business process of selling and how it could be altered by actually "seeing" the product or the impact. We began this section with Lowe's, who is using VR to sell the "new design," and TOMS, who is using VR to visualize the impact of buying a pair of shoes in the actual country where shoes are donated. These are not incremental innovations, but wholesale shifts.

2. **Product:** One big innovation area for product is in the way that AR/VR is used when a person's head is upright. Mobile phones today are limited in that people hold their head down. With AR/VR, the person's head can be upright. This simple change could extremely impact the innovation of the next generation of products. For example, at the recent Women of VR event that Facebook hosted, I reviewed business dashboards with my head upright, which enabled me to manipulate and organize groups of data together in different combinations. It visualized the data in ways I had never seen before. And, of course, then there are games. Gaming is being changed forever by AR/VR.

3. **Operational:** Some of the top operational innovation use cases for AR/VR are around training and maintenance, from flight simulators to train pilots, to training photographers, maintenance workers, and people in educational institutions. One company is developing AR technology for commercial printer repair. The solution would eliminate the number of service calls by training the person who owns the printer to do their own repairs.

4. **Customer Experience:** Since AR/VR can simulate and measure the reaction of customers to new designs and products, customer experiences can be innovated using AR/VR to measure (combined with IoT) the reaction to a variety of features. Sephora is doing this today with their virtual reality makeup artists.

Extreme Innovation

AR/VR will disrupt most industries going forward, not just gaming.

Games

Advertising

Film/News

Health/
Wellness

Education

Enterprise

Retail

Social

(Revised image used with permission from Dave Curry, VP
Emerging Trends & Technology, POP)

In Collaboration with the SmartVizx Team Monami Mitra, Kunal Grover, Gautam Tewari, and Tithi Tewari

Case Study: How SmartVizx Is Leveraging VR to Innovate

SmartVizX is India's leading virtual reality solutions company that is disrupting traditional passive and static design visualization methodologies. They do this by creating high quality Virtual Reality based across platform solutions that are immersive, interactive, and engaging. Currently catering to the AEC (Architecture, Engineering, and Construction) industry, SmartVizX has over 20 clients including reputed brands such as Developer Group, DASNAC, RockWorth, NIIT, The Quint, Interglobe Aviation, Express Avenue and Express Group etc., and is growing at over 100% Year on Year (YoY).

SmartVizX has developed a comprehensive suite of VR-based cross-platform products and a set of custom services that help companies target the most complex of issues in the Design and Build cycle.

(Revised image used with permission from SmartVizX)

SmartVizX helps its clients successfully market their projects prior to the actual construction. Imagine being able to roam around and view the interiors of a flat, or be able to peek beneath furniture and fixtures, check out different flooring materials and more, simply by wearing a VR Headset. SmartVizx provides this capability today by rendering a building even before its foundation has been laid in the real world.

Why is this important? Apart from the sheer innovativeness of the entire experience, a VR walkthrough or more importantly, a VR-led Design and Build approach—ensures accurate product representation to a potential customer, minimizes errors in construction, and reduces the possibility of expensive re-work.

SmartVizX has delivered high impact solutions to over 20 clients since its inception. Ranging from industries such as real estate to manufacturing, the company's VR products have generated quantifiable outcomes for its clients.

Some of the successful examples include:

- **Electromech Material Handling Systems India Pvt Ltd:** Asia's largest industrial crane manufacturer, Electromech faced a unique problem. Attracting business was a costly and time consuming exercise involving costly business trips that had to be arranged for national and international customers. SmartVizX's 360-VIZ solution provided a comprehensive tour of the company's capabilities in a convenient but immersive and informative VR-based format. This helped Electromech win international contracts without incurring any of the earlier costs due to expensive travel and delays in decision making.

- **BMR Advisors:** A corporate interiors project, this task for BMR Advisors saw deployment of a one of a kind solution from SmartVizX; VR Aided Build, or VRAB. BMR Advisors is a professional services firm which offers a range of tax, risk, and M&A advisory services for domestic and global businesses spanning several industries. The job here was to re-furbish and re-design the company's new 25,000 square foot office in Bengaluru. The use of VRAB here meant that the entire project was designed in VR first before the actual construction began. Through the use of VRAB, not only was the move-in of the project achieved on time, but shortfalls in inventory were also identified beforehand, potentially saving thousands of dollars.

SmartVizx has learned several lessons while developing a leading edge solution that uses VR to help clients innovate. Several items to think about are:

- **One size does not fit all:** VR being an evolving technology, there is no standard solution that meets requirements of clients across sectors and geographies. There is a strong need to develop products that transcend the challenges of hardware and internet bandwidths. This learning led the company to develop a wide selection of cross-platform VR-based products that could run on the most portable as well as most sophisticated of devices.

- **Customization is the key:** Developing cross-platform solutions is simply the first step to solving the problem. The only way to make VR work for everyone is to identify each unique problem and develop a custom VR solution based on the existing product portfolio. No two companies are the same, and therefore no two solutions can be the same.

- **VR needs to be budget friendly to be a viable alternative:** If VR-based technologies are to become mainstream, they need to fit the client's budget. SmartVizX therefore carefully executes each project to ensure maximum cost efficiency to be able to offer sophisticated VR-based solutions at competitive prices.

- **One can never stop innovating:** Given that there are no specific barriers to entry in this space if one possesses the right technological capabilities, it is crucial to keep innovating in order to maintain an edge over competition. SmartVizX therefore invested in a dedicated R&D center after the very first year of its inception. It has built a highly talented team comprised of senior professionals in the VR industry who now focus on new product development and refinement of existing solutions.

VR continues to be in evolution. The hardware is changing even as people are discovering uses of the technology. New forms of content are emerging. The first proper VR cinematic experience, *Miyubi* by Felix and Paul Studios, is now out. Sectors as varied as healthcare to defense establishments are developing content and applications based on VR technology. However, VR itself has a long way to go before it becomes a way of life.

One of the biggest challenges remains the technology itself. Good hardware is expensive and lower-priced variants are yet to completely meet the frame rate requirements key to a true VR experience. A normal feature film runs at 30 frames per second, but a VR needs to run at 90 frames per second per eye, which is essentially three times that of a typical cinematic experience. Poor quality hardware also means that a comfortable VR experience is not available for a majority of users, which again is a constraint with respect to mass adoption of the technology. Last but not the least, the usual 2D graphic user interfaces make little sense in a VR environment, while the common input devices like mouse and keyboards become irrelevant.

However, AR/VR are poised to become game-changers in an already technologically advanced world. Both of these technologies have the potential to permanently change the way human beings communicate with each other. Exceptionally relevant to situations and circumstances that require visualization tools, AR/VR will replace the usual charts, spreadsheets, images, video, etc. that we currently rely upon as visualization support.

AR/VR will become integral to education, healthcare, military, entertainment, manufacturing, and countless other industries. They will help simulate dangerous situations, build better scientific models, and essentially become the new formats of content consumption.

[Thanks to the SmartVizx Team for your expert advice.]

Shel Israel
Author with Robert Scoble of *The Fourth Transformation*

The best way to get started with VR/AR in an innovation realm:

- **Think universally.** Over the next five to ten years, mixed reality technologies will pervade almost everything—yes, everything—from retail, healthcare, education, logistics, and design to entertainment, communications, travel, financial services, and art. VR will be used to decorate your hotel room to your personal tastes. This is the time to think long and big. The drivers of mixed reality technologies are changing the world. If you don't have a dream to do that and if you are not willing to pay the price to make that dream come true, then don't bother. Get a job for someone who does. The best ideas change things, even if they appear small, such as giving people rides that are better than the experience of taxis.

- **Look Forward.** These new changes are more dynamic than ever before for the tech sector. Don't look for established procedures or best practices. There aren't any, and for a while and there won't be any. Get a sense of the players, products, technologies, and investment dollars in your sector of focus. Look at where it is today, then make your best possible guess at where you will be on the day you expect to have a product. If you cannot get in front of the current leader, then find another sector.

Look forward culturally as well. Very often, businesses don't look forward demographically. You need to see your customers as Millennials and the next generation of digital natives who are now in high school and even younger. Five years from today they will be your customers, new employees, and competitors. Speak their language and think as they do.

- **Think of users first.** This has been a flaw of too many companies over too many years. They fall in love with technology then invest in trying to persuade people to use it. The smart strategy is to look at the people first and figure out how you can make technology that will improve some aspect of their lives in a way that supports your financial model.

  For merchants and brands, your biggest challenge in the next five years is to get ahead of your customers, so that you are the best competitors in providing new experiences—experience that are memorable and worth talking about. In the next era, the experience will be the marketing program.

Perils:

If you are a technologist or an entrepreneur, there can also be perils. AR/VR already has many of the world's best minds, backed by the world's deepest pockets competing fiercely for a very nascent market. The likes of Apple, Google, Amazon, Microsoft, and Facebook are already vying for share in a market that is not yet formed. If you want to contribute to AR/VR, you need to have a really good idea and an absolutely awesome team.

If you are a major brand, you need to consider that whatever products you adopt today will be obsolete by tomorrow. However, increasingly, your customers, employees, and partners will expect to use AR/VR when dealing with you.

Chapter 7

[Thanks Shel for your expert advice.]

Get Smarter:

I'd highly recommend the book *Fourth Transformation* by Robert Scoble and Shel Israel.

CHAPTER 8

Super Intelligence using Blockchain

Introduction: What is Blockchain?

Monique Morrow
Chief Technology Strategist

Blockchain technology is best known as the underlying technology that makes the Bitcoin digital asset and payment system possible. The technology was developed from a paper[39] written by an unidentified person named Satoshi Nakamoto, describing a robust, cryptographically secure, peer-to-peer mechanism for verifying transactions and preventing double-spending and corruption using proof-of-work[1] as a consensus tool.

Bitcoin was one of the first applications to leverage Blockchain technology.

Blockchain's innovation is trust, not money.

Elevator Pitch:

In essence, a Blockchain is a cryptographically secure record, or ledger, of digital events that is distributed (shared among many different parties). It can only be updated by consensus of most of the participants in the system—participants being compute "nodes" that are part of a particular

Blockchain network. Once a "block" of transactions is validated and entered into the "chain" (the "block-chain!"), the transaction information can never be erased.[40]

This sounds like a simple concept, but it provides a mechanism for amazing innovation in the digital world.

Blockchains remove the need for central trusted authorities on interactions online, thereby providing true decentralization of networks. Trusted third parties could include your bank providing you a statement, or an email service provider stating a message was delivered. If these third parties provide incorrect data (or our personal data to others), or are hacked, manipulated. or corrupted, it leads to huge problems, highlighting why security of the Internet is a disaster today.

Having a truly decentralized network based on a trusted model and distributed consensus on all transactions and events is revolutionary and can provide answers to many of the past trust problems of the existing digital world.

Blockchain technology has the potential to lead to a fully decentralized world based on trusted models, bringing a next generation of web architectures and applications with it.

Key Terms:

There are different types of Blockchains: Public, Private, and Community.

- **Public Blockchains** can be leveraged by anyone willing to pay the small cost to store transaction data on the Blockchain or to validation transactions for reward (usually in cryptocurrency like Bitcoins, a process known as "mining").

- **Private Blockchains** are closed for use by a single entity, be that a person or an enterprise. Private chains are useful, as they do not need to store the outside world's transactions on the private chain or demand a cost for users to store transaction data.
- **Community Blockchains** follow the same concept as private chains, expect several different entities may agree to share it.
- **Sidechains:** Private and Community Blockchains in the future may become Sidechains to a Public Blockchain. A Sidechain would be "two-way pegged" to a Public Blockchain—for example, Bitcoin's Blockchain—and allow cryptocurrency to be transferred between the two Blockchains, kind of like changing dollars to pounds sterling and back, depending on the Blockchain in which a transaction occurs. Sidechains are a relatively new area of Blockchain innovation, but have the potential to expand the already large number of feasible Blockchain use cases and be a real instigator for bringing Blockchain technology to the mainstream.
- **Shared Ledger.** An open way to share data where two parties can record a transaction efficiently, verifiably, and permanently.

Blockchain and Today's Digital World

The Blockchain market is growing rapidly across venture capital backed startups, established vendors and industry consortiums, and across industries. To date, over $1 billion has been invested into Blockchain related startups[41], with investment growth at 94% year on year.[42]

Startup industry sectors include financial—in the form of eWallets, payments, escrow, exchanges, and more—IoT, social media, and entertainment, including music streaming.

With the venture capital led startups being distributed across 23 countries, it is truly a worldwide, cross-market, digital phenomenon.

But the expansion of the Blockchain market is not limited to startups. Established technology vendors are also entering the market. This is reflected in the efforts of Microsoft's increasingly abundant Blockchain services on their Azure public cloud[43].

There are also several cross-industry consortiums investigating Blockchain technology, from the Linux foundation's Hyperledger[44] to more market specific initiatives such as the consortium of over 40 global banks and financial institutions backing the R3CEV company[45]

Blockchain and Finance

As Bitcoin, currency, and asset transactions were the original use case behind Blockchain technology, it is obvious that Blockchain, until recently, has been associated most heavily with the finance industry.

The use of Blockchain for financial transactions could potentially render a lot of existing centralized financial institution functionality redundant, and offer ways for banks to massively optimize some of the processes and reduce touchpoints and middlemen that transactions require to-day.

For this reason, financial institutions are heavily re-searching Blockchain technology and how its application can benefit how they currently operate, and how they can remain relevant to consumers in a world where Blockchain based functionality becomes more reliable.

Blockchain and IoT

Blockchain technology provides a means for the IoT to scale to the hundreds of billions of connected devices that are forecasted to emerge in the next 10 years.

By creating smart systems built on Blockchains, a crypto-secure ledger of all interactions between devices, web ser-vices, and humans can be maintained via direct communi-cation, without the need network (fog computing), or even within the devices themselves. This will enable smart de-vices to talk to other smart devices as independent agents. Smart devices could conduct all manner of transactions au-tomatically—such as a car that can diagnose, schedule, and pay for maintenance all by itself, or appliances that only run when the unit price of electricity is cheap enough.

Show me the Money – Profit:

At a macro level, Blockchain creates a value singularity around identity, security, relationships, and trust. It creates a single view of an entire data set.

Imagine vehicle maintenance with Blockchain. It opens the ability to capture provenance of each component part in a complex system that is otherwise hard to track. Smart contracts with Blockchain have several concrete use cases in land claims and in oil and mining for trans-border compliance.

[Thanks Monique for your expert advice.]

Blockchain will have an impact on extreme innovation. From the "Unlocking Economic Advantage with Blockchain" report: "Our view is that blockchain's impact may eventually reshape market structure, product capabilities and the client experience, ultimately having a lasting influence on the global economic system."[46]

Blockchain is driving all four types of innovation

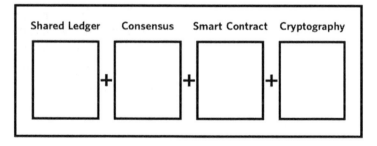

Blockchain is driving all four types of innovation

Shared Ledger + Consensus + Smart Contract + Cryptography

As we read above, Blockchain is a combination of a shared ledger consensus, smart contracts, and cryptography, and we can see Blockchain's broad and wide impact on extreme innovation. Here are some examples.

Business Process: Blockchain may be relatively new, but it is disrupting every industry—not just financial services. For example, a company called Follow My Vote is using Blockchain as their backbone for a secure online voting system to change the way that voting is done.

Product: Extreme innovative products are popping up globally. In a recent pitch competition, I saw a host of products built on Blockchain for ownership. For example, a newly designed product called Vault OS was developed by a group called Thought Machine. The product enables banks to deliver end to end secure financial systems.

Operational: There are several startups built on Blockchain who are looking to disrupt. For instance, a startup called Slock.it, which allows you to rent, sell, or share anything without intermediaries. Examples include wifi routers rented on demand, unused office spaces that can be rented, and more. They are trying to operationalize, automatically, the renting and selling process.

Customer Experience: For an extreme customer experience, most examples come from the peer-to-peer area. Imagine the new experience from a startup named BTCJam, who provides a lending service that is peer to peer, so that people from around the world can connect to borrow and lend seamlessly.

This is an exciting new area for innovation. This quote from everis NEXT embodies the spirit of the extremeness of Blockchain: "What is revolutionary about this technology is that the decentralized consensus breaks the old paradigm of centralized consensus (when one central database used to rule transaction validity). New flows of value can be created based on this consensus which sets new **legal and regulatory frameworks.**"[47]

Get Smarter:

I'd highly recommend the book *Blockchain Revolution* (2016), written by father and son team Don and Alex Tapscott.

New Roles as a Result of Super Intelligence

- **Meet the new Data Driven CEO:** The foundation for an extreme intelligence is real time information. CEOs will need to become more data-driven in order to pivot, leapfrog, and serve their customers. By 2020, over 40 billion things will connect to the internet.[48] This data lake can be a pot of gold. The new data-driven CEO will create a culture of data mining and exploration.

Meet the new Ambidextrous CMO: With all the new technology coming fast and furious, Chief Marketing Officers will have to not only understand marketing, but will hunger for big data to fuel their customer obsession, demand AI to analyze and predict the next big campaign, and mandate AR/VR to measure customer reactions. For example, even today publishers are offering capabilities for behaviorally programmatic targeting of premium advertising. Long ago a mentor advised me to earn a B.S. degree in computer science, and a masters in marketing and business, and he could not have been more right about this killer combination.

Meet the new Digital Prophet: With lily pads emerging frequently and at an increased pace, the new Digital Prophet will be able to use big data and technology to guide new extreme innovations. Like having a crystal ball, a person dedicated to pulling all the pieces together, assisted by machine learning, will help large companies get back into the innovation game. This represents an advantage over the small nimble startup, as the amount of data aids in your learning and intelligence, and the larger the organization, typically the bigger the data. Make sure you don't miss this one.

- **Meet the new Captain of Innovation Exploration**: Leveling up on the Vice President of Innovation role of today is the new Captain of Innovation Exploration. This person will be like Captain Kirk on the *Star Trek* Enterprise, exploring new lands and innovations unseen. Innovation will be global, so it will be essential to have someone running hackathons globally, as well as bootcamps and pitch competitions. Opening innovation outposts will also be essential to increase your super intelligence.

Super intelligence is a crucial superpower, but needs to be combined with super speed and super synergy. In the next chapters, a deep dive in these two areas will reveal how these powers work together.

I went deep and personal on super intelligence because it is the superpower that has changed the landscape of innovation the most. It requires a broad and well understood story that you can use to understand and implement the full context of all the ideas in this book.

CHAPTER 9
Super Speed: Cognitive Diversity

SUPER SPEED

Create Agility

- ✓ Chief Cultural Strategist
- ✓ Guru of Cognitive Diversity
- ✓ Chief Agility Officer

Cognitive Diversity

Cognitive diversity is-the most underrated element of extreme innovation,—because it's a talent element. Talent means people, and people cannot be measured by data normally used in business plans. Most businesses miss this when planning for innovation and creating innovation strategies. Cognitive diversity is underrated—not by intention, but because the value added by people of diverse backgrounds and talent are not considered part of innovation and innovation strategies. This is the one area where planners do not allocate money-to areas where the data can be measured and-the value accounted for.

Businesses in Silicon Valley operate on the model I've presented as extreme innovation. However, if you dig deeper into the experiential data under the category of cognitive diversity, you will find what I like to call the "shadow component" or the "hidden jewel" in thriving corporate cultures that are extreme innovators.

Cognitive diversity may provide the most opportunity to aquire talent and build a team that can be designed for breadth and depth of diversity. You are free to explore worldwide for people who could, in the right combination, take a company through every stage of extreme innovation at the speeds I have told you are necessary for success.

Ironically, if you ask anyone in technology what their number one problem is, they'll likely tell you that it is the challenge of trying to find talent.

Up next is the proof that cognitive diversity might be the sleeper in the shadows waiting to be woken up. I will share with you the latest thinking on cognitive diversity, as well as case studies that helped me realize the idea that cognitive diversity is probably the most underrated element of extreme innovation. There is, to my knowledge, no study of this idea, but by extrapolation of the current data and some magic I think we have uncovered a powerful new idea. See! The ability to offer understanding of extreme innovation requires having the qualities of an extreme innovator in the first place!

This is the fun in extreme innovation. Now let's take a look at some proof that cognitive diversity is valuable and should not be underrated, and that investing in a great talent pool of people from diverse backgrounds works.

I'll never forget the night I went to The Crunchies in San Francisco, an awards ceremony that recognizes and celebrates the most compelling startups that are winning the technology innovations of the year. When companies win, most send up their CEO to accept the award. But when I attended and Slack won for Fastest Rising Startup, they sent up a team of engineers who were all women representing a diversity in age, ethnicity, and style. This company made a bold statement by giving recognition to the people who cre ated value and were part of diversity team in innovation. They valued cognitive diversity. It was a statement about the value of diversity in innovation: cognitive diversity

Elevator Pitch:

Cognitive diversity is about the diversity of ideas and experiences of people from diverse backgrounds, and the value this brings into a team within a company. Gender and ethnicity are usually the two areas that spring to mind when talking about diversity, but cognitive diversity is much broader. Cognitive diversity could mean choosing team members from very different educational and social backgrounds, different worldviews, sexual orientation, and so forth.

Neil Lenane, Business Leader of Talent Management for Progressive Insurance, said that "If you do not intentionally include, you unintentionally exclude", which is essentially what cognitive diversity tries to achieve by bringing together people with differences in mental process, judgement, perception, and categorization.

Cognitive diversity has been shown to improve employee performance, enhance employee collaboration, increase employee workplace satisfaction, and increase innovation. It has also provided many useful insights into customer behaviors, which has allowed businesses to tailor their customer responses for better revenue generation while building customer loyalty.

But just forming the diverse team isn't the end all be all. Diverse teams must find ways to work together productively, and often the best ways of working may seem, at first, counterintuitive.

Hence, incorporating cognitive diversity in teams benefits extreme innovation. The Harvard Business Review article "Diverse Teams Feel Less Comfortable — and That's Why They Perform Better" runs through numerous research reports that showcase the powerful impact of diverse teams.[49] Based on numerous reports, we can see that higher revenues, more clients, more successful innovations, and even stronger profits come from diversity of thought.

In cognitive diversity, extreme innovators look for diversity in:

- Age—both Millennials and those over 50
- Gender (we will cover this later in the book)
- Many other areas, such as sexual orientation

The extreme innovators look for new ways to find that culture fit (like job shadowing marketplaces) and where talent is hiding (returners!)

Let's now focus on the new areas for acceleration. This chapter is structured in two sections: one focusing on how to find a culture fit, and the other on how to find hidden talent.

Hire "Returners" To Accelerate Extreme Innovation

Diane Flynn, CEO of Reboot Accelerator, is an amazing leader. She and a team of four women (Chrissie Kremer, Kristin Vais, Beth Kawasaki, and Patty White) had the innovative idea to start a company to help those wanting to re-enter the workforce after a pause from their career. She had innovation superpowers. Below is her story and expert advice.

Diane Flynn
CEO, Reboot Accelerator

Returning to Work

It was August 2014 and I sat in my team meeting on my first day of work. Terms were thrown around I had never heard before: Slack, SEO, pivot tables, hashtags (which I always thought were pound signs), and growth hacking. People were adding meetings to my calendar without asking my availability. And I didn't have 500 connections on LinkedIn—I didn't even have a LinkedIn profile. How had I got here?

Chapter 9

I hold a Stanford degree in Economics and a Harvard MBA. I had a successful career at the Boston Consulting Group and was a senior marketing exec at Electronic Arts for a decade. Then I decided to pause my career. I had two toddlers at home who I felt needed my attention, and a third with medical issues. Something had to give. Little did I realize that I would pause my career for over 15 years. During this time, I stayed engaged. I served on boards, chaired marketing committees for nonprofits, and was an advisor to the Stanford Children's Hospital where my son had numerous surgeries. Few of these were paid activities, but they filled my life with purpose and meaning.

I am among the 2.3 million women each year who have paused their careers and want to return to the workforce. In fact, 90% of moms who pause would like to re-enter, but most find it challenging given their outdated workplace tech skills, lack of professional connections, and diminished confidence. So in 2015, I co-founded ReBoot Accel, aimed at getting women current, connected, and confident to return. Our program has been wildly successful, and after 18 months has expanded to major cities throughout the US. What a thrill it's been catalyzing women to explore their next path and navigate new careers. And it's been a boon to forward-thinking companies interested in tapping into this incredible pool of fresh, energized talent.

Elevator Pitch: How Exactly Can Hiring Those Who Have "Paused" Their Career Impact Innovation?

Companies must consider hiring those who've paused their careers. These women—and, increasingly, men—are as ambitious, educated, and experienced as the Millennials that often fill open positions. And they often have lower training costs, higher retention, and bring with them valuable experience, connections, stability, maturity, and ability to get things done. They add both gender and age diversity to the workforce, something we know drives innovation. Research shows teams led by women grow faster and have higher return on investment (ROI's). Companies with female executives are more profitable, and teams with a wider range of work backgrounds produce more innovative products.

Key Terms:

a) **Paused Career:** We encourage those who've stepped out of the workforce to call it a "pause." They haven't stopped, dropped out, or retired. They have made a conscious decision to make something else a priority for a period of time—whether that be six months or 20 years. Some are caring for young children, others for aging parents, or perhaps an ailing spouse.

b) **Returnship:** A low-risk program for both employers and "returners" to check each other out. The employer benefits by "trying out" talent who have extensive experience but may need to update their skills. The returner gets to see if the company is a fit while on-ramping their skills and network. It's a low-risk, low-cost program to let both sides determine if there's a long-term fit.

c) **Returner:** One who has paused their career and is now returning to the paid workforce, whether part-time, full-time, or with an entrepreneurial venture.

Case Study: JetBlue Technology Ventures

Meet Dana Posey. Dana has an MBA and an engineering degree. She worked in the Electric Power Industry for over a decade. She then made the complicated decision to pause her career for over 15 years. After deciding to re-enter the workforce, she enrolled in ReBoot Accel, where she learned today's workplace skills, developed a professional network, and developed the confidence needed to return. After completing ReBoot, she interned with us for four months to gain confidence and hone her skills. Pivoting to Corporate Venture Capital, she applied for a job with JetBlue Technology Ventures managing their office. One of nine candidates in the interview process, she was chosen for the job. After talking to the hiring manager who ran the venture, it was clear that Dana's experience, judgment, confidence, maturity, and ability to get things done as a result of being a multitasking mom made her the preferred candidate. Dana was a significant contributor immediately, and her experience and knowledge brought a different and important perspective to the team. She received a promotion after only nine months on the job and is now the Operations Manager for the Corporate Venture Capital firm. She is in the process of hiring another ReBoot graduate to work with her—talk about a full-circle moment.

Show me the Money – Profit:

While returners sometimes have the stigma of being dinosaurs, they are actually great for the bottom line. Three factors work in the company's favor: 1) reduced training costs; 2) higher retention, and thus lower costs of recruiting; and 3) lower initial salaries.

New employees typically take six months to recover the recruitment and training costs. Hiring returners who have held these positions takes significantly less time. Millennials believe they will be in a job for just under two years; returners plan to stay on five years or more, due to greater insights into their passions, more stability, and the fact that they're usually not subject to maternity leaves and spousal relocations. In high-cost areas, they can also have lower relocation costs because they often live in the area and own homes. Shorter commutes can mean more time in the office, greater job satisfaction, and higher retention. Because returners often need to update their skillsets, they can often be hired for below market compensation, at least initially. Returners generally advance at a rapid rate and often quickly achieve market compensation.

Change the World – Purpose:

Age-blended workplaces drive innovation. Not only that, but employees who have parented children have a unique worldview that influences products and services. My professional life was always filled with older, successful role models. At BCG, my mentor was Indra Nooyi, now CEO of Pepsi. She provided guidance, inspiration, and fought for me in partner meetings. Likewise, at Electronic Arts, I sought the wise counsel and mentorship of Nancy Smith, Senior VP of Sales. She provided counsel for me on how to navigate my career, effectively build my skillset, and establish credibility with senior management. My 24-year-old daughter says she always looks to older female role models for tips on leadership, how to hire and fire employees, and how to choose from myriad competing priorities.

We had 26 interns last summer at our company. With a skeletal staff, it's easy to lose focus on the program, resulting in the interns fending for themselves much of the time. But given my experience as a mom, having witnessed two daughters live through seven internships—some good, some horrific—I helped design a program that put the interns first. We had regular check-in's, provided shadowing opportunities for them to explore new positions, weekly lunches where CEOs shared their startup experiences, and end of internship report-outs to build presentation skills. I met with each of the interns on their last day to conduct an exit interview and see how I could help with their career plans through skill development, guidance, and connections. This perspective was largely driven by my experience as a mom and hearing tales from my daughters each day about the good, the bad, and the ugly at their internships. This is but one tiny example of how diverse perspectives shape the workplace and drive innovation.

Perils:

While returners can offer much to the workplace and drive innovation, it can be challenging balancing a multi-generational workforce. Returners are sometimes feared to be deficient. We encourage women in the ReBoot program to develop a "growth mindset" and constantly be willing to learn new skills. Today's workplace is one that requires life-long learning, and returners need to own their skill development by taking classes, watching YouTube videos, and Googling solutions. There needs to be sensitivity to the nuances of different generations, and an appreciation for how to work in unity and maximize impact.

Promises:

Multigenerational workforces full of cognitive diversity contribute to a rich and innovative culture. In addition, there are great opportunities for mentorship, sharing of real-world experience, and cross-training between generations. I have personally worked in workplaces where I've been both youngest and oldest, and both offer incredible opportunities for growth, mentorship, and skill development. To prepare our workforce for 2020 and beyond, we need to be open to a variety of viewpoints and experiences that add to our rich mosaic and drive innovation.

Offer **flexible schedules** to accommodate a broader labor pool

Develop **"returner" programs** to trial those who've paused

Add a "returner" to your **candidate pool**

[Thanks Diane for your expert advice.]

Job Shadowing – An Extreme Innovator Approach

Turnover is a huge cost to a company these days—around $50,000 per person—and that is just at an entry level. Turnover is also at its highest with Millennials unsatisfied with their jobs, and thus job-hopping. 65% of people look for a new job within 91 days of being hired into a company. Having to hire and rehire takes a toll on your company's culture and extreme innovative spirit.

Why is that? What happens is that most people don't understand in a typical interview what exactly the job really entails, what the day-to-day looks like, and what working there feels like. For Millennials in particular, the feel is very important. They often take the job, and then they quickly realize: *Nope, this isn't for me.*

Extreme innovators are finding new ways to determine people-company fit. One approach is job shadowing. By job shadowing a position first, candidates are given a much clearer mental picture of what that job really is and are much more likely to stay. This in turn will decrease turnover overall. In addition, we all know that tech companies in general are struggling to attract diversity, and job shadowing can showcase a company's commitment to be an inclusive culture.

Betagig, a Los Angeles startup we explored in Chapter 4, has created a marketplace for candidates and companies.

Students and job-seekers can use the job shadowing market-place to try out careers before making a commitment. Likewise, companies can use Betagig to try out potential candidates and hire from the job shadowers that fit them well. With Betagig's ratings and reviews system, a company can use job shadowing to get diversity in their doors, and also quickly figure out why they aren't attracting the right types of people. Betagig is helping companies reduce turnover andhiring costs, attract diversity and people to their brand in general.

The key here is that if everyone loves what they do, extreme innovators can create a more productive society on the whole. Everyone wants to feel like they are making an impact on something or someone with the work they do, especially Millennials—who will make up the majority of the workforce in just five years.

Everyone wants to feel part of something big. Innovative sourcing of talented people is based on creating the sizzle to attract and retain people from a diverse range of areas.

If your talent is allowed to explore and figure out not only which career, but also which company, makes them feel like they are making an impact and keeping them satisfied, then the economy will thrive, people won't be so complacent or unhappy in their jobs anymore, and work-related depression will decrease.

After all, we spend most of our adult lives working. We should enjoy what we're doing—and our work should be stimulating and rewarding.

This is the new brave world for looking for a great culture fit and great new talent!

Over 50 - Introduction:

In the 2015 film *The Intern,* Robert DeNiro plays an experienced business executive over the age of 50 who helps turn around a startup business with a female founder played by Anne Hathaway. This film offers a great view of the two demographics that can impact innovation: those over 50 and the up-and-coming Millennials.

Elevator Pitch: Diversity in Age – Over 50 Impact Innovation

Many people think that those over 50 are ready for retirement and cannot keep up in the workforce. But the data shows otherwise. According to the Wall Street Journal, there are more gains in the workforce from those over 55 than under 55. Workers over 50 comprise 33.4% of the US labor force, up from 25% in 2002, per BLS Statistics.[50]

Employers sometimes mistakenly assume older applicants are less creative, less productive, slower mentally, and more expensive to employ than early- or mid-career employees. They also feel they're not current in today's workplace technologies. How can these people innovate?

Peter Cappelli, a management professor at the Wharton School and coauthor (with former AARP CEO Bill Novelli) of *Managing the Older Worker,* explore all of the assumptions about those over 50 in their book. They pulled together research from psychology, demography, and even economics, and what they determined was that virtually none of these stereotypes holds up.

Recent research from AARP, "The surprising truth about older workers", shows that older workers score high in leadership, detail-oriented tasks, organization, listening, writing skills, and problem solving—even in cutting-edge fields like computer science.[51]

And we're finding that age-blended workplaces are the most effective in driving innovation, mentorship, and skills training. In fact, looking at entrepreneurs, more than 25% of new startups were started by those over the age of 55—up 16% from 1996. And—are you ready for this?—70% of startups founded by people aged 50 or older last longer than three years, versus 28% for those founded by people younger than 50, based on a report by researchers at City University of London's Cass Business School.[52]

Those extreme innovators like Regeneron, #3 on Forbes' Most Innovative Companies list,[53] have started internships for older workers. And they are not alone: others like McKinsey, the Harvard Business School, and Goldman Sachs have done the same. Already, Barclays has a team of tech-savvy older workers in place to help mature customers with online banking. They believe that a mixed workforce has the diversity needed to go to the next level.

Mixed workforces will have the best chances to innovate to the extreme.

Check out Encore.org, who have dedicated themselves to this up and coming new workforce.

Elevator Pitch: Diversity in Age – The Millennials

While the AARP argues for older workers, younger employees are also a valuable element in the workforce. They love to take risks and have innovation in their DNA. By 2020, *Millennials* will make up approximately 50% of the U.S. workforce, and by 2030, 75% of the global workforce.

Did you know that one in three American workers today are Millennials? They are now bigger than Gen X![54]

When Millennials enter the workforce, they consistently have a different set of goals and ideas about what a job should be. Many companies are having issues with recruiting and retention because of these differences. In addition, since Millennials will be big spenders as well as employees, focus on knowing this community is going to impact success. According to research by Accenture, by 2020, Millennial spending in the United States will grow to $1.4 trillion annually and represent 30% of total retail sales.

According to the 2016 Deloitte Millennial Survey "Winning Over the Next Generation of Leaders," two-thirds of Millennials express a desire to leave their organizations by 2020.[55] Businesses must adjust how they nurture loyalty among Millennials or risk losing a large percentage of their workforces that drives innovation. From the same research, Deloitte found that 60% of Millennials think their employers are innovative, but only half think their employer helps them to be innovative. 62% of Millennials describe themselves as innovative.

Their communication style is different and innovative as well. Some would say they love the "culture of emoji." Emojis don't just represent to the Millennials a smile or frown, but a feeling and emotion. Note, the first emoticon was sent in 1982 from Carnegie Mellon to indicate sarcasm in a text, and emojis originated in Japan. Companies are learning that Millennials communicate in this style—in fact, Domino's now even allows you to text a pizza emoji to order a pizza!

Age generally equates to experience. However, ideation and perspective comes from everywhere and in different ways of expression—like emojis! Inclusion is critical.

A great story from Allison Wiener, co-founder of the NextGen group at Clorox, was the difference in millennials' responses to their bosses sending text with a "Hello Allison" vs an "I could use your help" paired with a Smiley Face Emoji to open the conversation.

If you want millennials to express themselves, try using emojis as an extreme innovative communication style. I did an entire meeting where we only used emojis to communicate—much like a recent Chevy commercial that targeted the millennial crowd by having potential customers rate cars using emojis only!

When you are looking for diversity, you need to go beyond gender, ethnicity, and sexual orientation andlook at age as well.

In the Bay Area and beyond, the pace is lightning fast, so it is important to have different viewpoints built in. Having Millennials embedded in the process also broadens the perspective. Remember, Millennials are very connected. They live with roommates, go to many social outings, take the bus to work, and do bring a larger set of ideas from more diverse places than other age groups. According to CNN Money, on the last US Census, the Millennial generation was found to be bigger and more diverse than the Boomers.[56]

Some facts:

- 83% of Millennials want business to do more to help the future
- 78% recommend companies base on the good they do
- 69% of Millennials want their companies to make it easier for them to get involved in innovation[57]

Terms to Know:

- **Millennials:** Those who were born between 1980 and 2000.
- **Millenial Mindset:** According to WorkBright, the "Millennial Mindset" is a way of thinking that builds being socially conscious into all aspects of life. Millennials pay attention to where businesses spend their money and how they contribute to society as well as what the company sells.[58]
- **We>Me:** Collaboration is the future. Millennials think in terms of the greater good vs the individual.
- **Emoji:** A small digital image or icon used to express an idea, emotion, etc. in electronic communication.
- **Emojipedia:** An emoji search engine.
- **Reverse mentor:** Having a junior employee mentor someone more seasoned.

Case Study: The Clorox Company

Allison Wiener, co-founder of Clorox's NextGen group, is a leader in bringing networks together. When she graduated from California Polytechnic State University and began her role at Clorox, she found there was only one other millennial in her area. And while the campus was beautiful and large, she didn't really know anyone her age and felt a bit isolated.

As a millennial, Allison had a strong sense of wanting to matter and to contribute to Clorox's growth culture. At a lunch workout class, she met a few other millennials and began the discussion of their impact over a simple lunch.

But the lunch grew.

Soon around 50 millennials were meeting together for lunch – sometimes in the café or at In-and-Out burger to chat, share their stories and brainstorm. The group had become so large that Allison and another colleague decided that they – the next generation at Clorox – needed to be made formal.

With support from Erby Foster – who has been a driving force behind diversity and inclusion initiatives across Clorox, encouraging and empowering teams to take bold steps – arrangements were made for Allison to present to the Clorox People and Culture Team Committee. As the youngest person to ever present to the group of C-suite executives and diversity team members, Allison prepared ahead of time emphasizing the great return for Clorox in supporting and including this set of millennials.

The NextGen group won support from the committee and now is impacting the company beyond the lunches for community support.

Allison and the group have begun a reverse mentoring program with millennials mentoring executives and leaders across the company. In addition, they have begun providing input into the innovation of the future. While the NextGen group input doesn't replace the research that Clorox does, it impacts it in the beginning stages. According to Allison, the result is a group of millennials who feel empowered and included – two great morale indicators that the people might stick around.

In addition to furthering innovation and continuous learning, Allison was invited as part of the NextGen group to join a newly formed Data Science Team. Previously, this group was comprised of those with master's and PhD degrees. Being on this very diverse team has again emphasized that Clorox is embedding diversity into its DNA. Marketing leadership at Clorox asks Allison and her team regularly after conferences, or learning sessions, what they saw and what we could apply to our business. Leadership has implemented several of the millennial ideas.

This empowerment is what startups do so well to retain the next generation – and it is what Clorox is doing as well – embedding a startup culture inside of a big company.

Best Practices from Clorox:
- Have leaders who inspire and empower.
- Pick a Millennial with leadership and potential, and grow that leader for the movement

- Showcase impact beyond community. Innovation and Data Science are two hot areas where Clorox encouraged the involvement of NextGen, and the millennial group has made notable contributions.

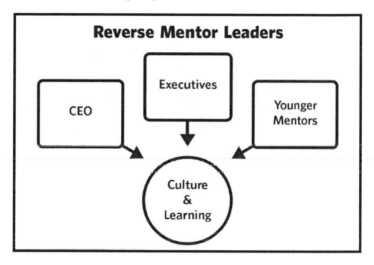

Brian Fanzo
CEO, iSocialFanz

How Millennials on Your Team Accelerate Innovation

The future of innovation is collaboration. Collaboration for Millennials is as natural and native as the idea of sharing one's knowledge with a colleague and working as a team to accomplish a common goal. Collaboration is just the standard way of getting things done for Millennials, as they've never felt limited by the place they live or the people they know; those kinds of limitations don't exist in a digitally connected world.

The rate of change today is happening at a speed we've never seen before. For most Millennials, this rate of change is not only exciting, but has become the new norm as the immediacy of technology rapidly being replaced is the new circle of life. Millennials' excitement for the speed of change, desire for open, transparent communication, and ability to seek collaborative communities to spur learning and sharing of knowledge prevents them from being overwhelmed by tighter timelines, pivoting deliverables, or exposure to competitor data.

Although collaboration is the heart of innovation in a Millennial's mind, collaboration is less about the technology that facilitates collaboration and more about streamlining communication with people who are willing to share and work in a transparent, cooperative culture.

Millennials believe so much in the power of collaboration that they're often willing to collaborate and be open to their competition, as long as it allows them to innovate faster and achieve the goals they're striving to accomplish. This collaborative approach to innovation requires project communication protocols to be clearly defined, and intellectual property or classified information identified and protected.

The millennial desire to feel and know that their voices are heard and that what they're doing is making a difference requires businesses and leadership to take a different approach to how innovation strategy is shared, incentivized, and celebrated within an organization.

Leaders today are often overwhelmed and become frustrated with Millennials because of their desire to be heard. On the other hand, there are leaders who are excited by Millennials because this younger generation's desire to know what they're working on is making an impact. Rather than being frustrated.

Leaders can increase the speed of innovation by providing a method for open communication and transparent collaboration. This increase happens because Millennials aren't afraid to fail or have their ideas rejected. This lack of fear in this regard generally occurs as a byproduct of open communication and transparent collaboration amongst peers, empowering the leader to focus on the current task while tapping into these innovative ideas when the time is right.

Millennials don't have to look outside the box for creative ideas, as they've never understood why there was a box in the first place—hence their willingness to question the status quo without hesitation or preconceived ideas. Millennials' enthusiasm for change, desire to make a difference, and willingness to fail fast and learn even more quickly will be a massive accelerator of innovation when empowered by leadership within a trusting, innovative culture.

[Thanks Brian for your expert advice.]

Let's Get This Party Started:

Innovation is best served with a cognitively diverse team: Millennials, returners, and those more experienced all working together to solve the world's problems. There is a war for talent, and having the best possible teams accelerates your focus.

As a business leader, to optimize extreme innovation, consider the following:

1. Business leaders can start by expanding their vision of what makes a great employee. It's not always the newly minted college graduate or the experienced Millennial; often, those who've paused and return to the workforce offer wisdom, mentorship, maturity, stability, and common sense that can prove valuable. Not only that, but their often-reduced starting salaries, lower training costs, and higher retention are all meaningful to the bottom line.

2. For business leaders to take advantage of a Millennial approach to innovation, they first must determine the problem, define what success looks like, and allow for everyone in the group to share their opinions and preliminary work in a transparent setting that is free from judgement before a formal program and process is carried out.

3. Business leaders must acknowledge that innovating and collaborating are not solutions or methodologies that can be turned on or off within a team, a company, or a community. It's an evolving give and

take process, and it is important to continually learn to become a unique team.

4. Team leadership is not determined by the title of those on the team; rather, it is based on finding the person who best fits the current problem to expedite the best path to resolution.

5. Hire blended teams, not those that all look alike. But most importantly, recognize and embrace the differences. Advice from the Harvard Business School shows that celebrating differences gets teams working more collaboratively together.

6. Provide mentors and encourage mentorship for all, especially returners and Millennials. Ensure you are providing constant feedback and encourage experimentation.

7. Implement reverse mentoring with Millennials.

8. Throw a returner into your hiring pool. See how she (or he) does! They're easy to find, now that many programs exist to help those who've paused, like Re-Boot Accel, who have thousands of members and are expanding nationally.

9. Develop a program specifically for returners. Offer a 12-week internship that lets these individuals prove their merit while you get a chance to check out the cultural and workplace fit. It's a low-cost way to find new, energized talent.

10. Post your jobs on the many job boards targeting returners. These include ReBoot Accel, Apres, Encore.org, Manera Solutions, Talent Reconnect, MomCorps, and Maybrooks.

11. Communications in the blended workforce can be tricky. Test and experiment with variety. For instance, learn emoji speak!
12. Experiment with job shadowing as an extreme approach to showcasing your culture-people fit.

Now that we have a cognitively diverse workforce, we need to grow the talent in new ways. Like our pond full of lily pads, talent grows the culture and drives extreme innovation. Our next chapter discusses how to drive a continuous learning culture.

CHAPTER 10
Super Speed: Continuous Learning Culture of Mentoring

I'll never forget reading *Alice in Wonderland* to my children. There was a section of the book that was especially significant:

> "My dear, here we must run as fast as we can, just to stay in place. And if you wish to go anywhere you must run twice as fast as that."

Lewis Carroll, *Alice in Wonderland*

Speed matters.

Innovation is happening faster today than it ever has in the past. As a result, you have to run twice as fast.

From the best practices that I have seen, speed is deceiving. Things that you think would slow you down actually, in the end, speed you up.

Culture, cognitive diversity, and processes aren't things that you'd naturally associate with speed. Yet when you dig deeper, they buy you extra horsepower to cross the line sooner.

Culture

Elevator Pitch:

The best of the best always mention culture as a key to winning in the innovation game. Culture is the environment consisting of experiences, beliefs, values, attitudes, and customs that define a company.

From Forbes' recent Most Innovative Companies list, the top companies attribute culture to their success in innovation:

- "Tesla Motors, Inc.'s organizational culture creates human resource competence necessary for innovative products in the automotive business. A firm's organizational or corporate *culture* represents the customs and values that define workers' behaviors and decision-making."[59]
- Salesforce attributes its innovative nature to the spirit of Aloha that is found throughout the company.
- From Regeneron: "At Regeneron, we believe in the power of original thinking. Our company culture is built on breakthrough ideas, which is why we foster a spirit of openness, and strive to inspire from within. We are collaborative by design and driven by curiosity."[60]
- UnderArmour's culture is built on making all athletes better through passion, design, and the relentless pursuit of innovation.[61]

Essentially, corporate cultures are built on innovation by everybody with rapid feedback. Collaboration is high. But I want to go beyond what you can read in lots of other books and hone in on one of the secrets of extreme innovation. Extreme innovation companies have a culture built on lifetime learning and mentors. I am not talking about mentoring in the golden age way, but mentoring in the next century at lightning speed. Mentoring is a vital part of an extreme innovation culture.

Show me the Money – Profit:

Endeavor Insight analysis did a study of 700 startups. Given the size of their base, they could compare these founders with those that were top performing. They defined a criterion of top performing based on successful exit, scale, and investor traction. They uncovered an interesting pattern. To quote the report: "We found that many of the entrepreneurs leading these startups had strong personal connections to the founders of other successful companies. One of the most powerful connections identified in our analysis was mentoring relationships."[62] In fact, they found that those with strong mentoring relationships were three times more successful than those that did not have these relationships.

Percentage of Companies That Are Top Performers

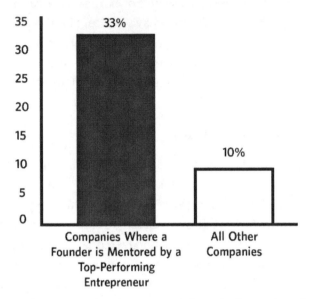

(Revised image used with permission from Endeavor Insights)

Peer to peer mentoring is part of the superpowers of innovation. But it is not just for entrepreneurs. In a recent Forbes article, it was noted how Toyota suffered from a lack of mentors. They claimed it had a directly negative effect on the brand. After rapid expansion, they did not have enough mentors, and their innovation suffered.[63]

Change the World – Purpose:

Deloitte recently performed a Millennial Survey, and here are the facts for the next generation workforce that they found:

- 94% of Millennials believe that mentors are essential to their success.

- 68% of Millennials who wanted to stay with their company had a mentor, compared with 32% of those who did not. Millennials believe that mentors help them to grow and innovate in new ways.[64]

Mentoring to Accelerate Innovation

Rajesh Setty, Founder of MentorCloud, is one of my all-time favorite mentors. He co-founded MentorCloud because of his intense belief in its impact on innovation in a culture. Below are some of his thoughts on why mentoring is part of fostering an extreme innovator culture.

***

Rajesh Setty
Founder, MentorCloud

In today's world where change is happening at an unprecedented speed, innovation is about bringing the right ideas to life—ideas that are in sync with the current state of reality or those that set your company up to take advantage of what's coming in the near future. My friend Stephen Shapiro, author of *24/7 Innovation*, says "innovation is simply staying relevant."

The genesis of any innovation is an insight. One has an insight when he or she sees something different from everyone that is around him or her. They spot an opportunity hidden in plain sight. It was always there for everyone to see, but this person sees what everybody else missed seeing.

Sadly, most of these insights die a natural death in the minds of those people without ever seeing the light of the day. For every idea that becomes a reality, a thousand of them go straight to the grave.

By simply increasing the odds of your employees bringing novel ideas to life that are relevant to today's marketplace, your company can unlock a fortune.

How can your company do that? Good question.

Before we get there, let us first see why most ideas take the fastest path from the cradle to the grave.

Why Most Innovative Ideas Encounter a Premature Death

There are many different reasons that most innovative ideas encounter a premature death, such as the innovator jumping too quickly to another shiny idea, or the marketplace changing further to make that idea irrelevant.

If I had to choose the most common reason, it would be the lack of access to the right kind of help at all stages to make measurable progress in reasonable time.

Let's think about this for a minute. First, any meaningful quest requires good help because of the nature and magnitude of what you are going after. Why? Simply because, however smart someone is, they alone may not be sufficient to do everything to take that innovative idea and bring it to life in a timeframe that will make it happen within the "window of relevance." In a fast-moving world, the "window of relevance" is fast-shrinking.

So. where do employees get good help in a timely fashion?

The Power of Mentoring

Building a mentoring network where your employees have access to an internal (and external, if it makes sense) network of mentors is a good starting point to give your employees the right kind of timely help.

A mentor is someone who is not only competent in their relevant craft, but also cares enough for you to invest their time and energy to take you to the next level.

Note that a mentor is not someone to whom one will delegate their problem, but someone because of whom one will increase their own capacity to solve that problem or to rise up to the challenge.

My friend Ravi Gundlapalli, founder of MentorCloud and the author of the book *The Art of Mentoring*, says that mentoring works because it's learning in context from a domain expert who you also respect. Context is the key word here.

When someone has an insight that is the seed of an innovative idea, a mentoring conversation helps them get out of what I call "idea inertia" (enormous friction that is stopping someone from getting off the starting block).

Why? Because one or more focused conversations with a mentor helps the creator to ask the following questions and more:

- How can they clarify their own idea?
- How can they reflect on whether the idea is really innovative or an also-ran?

- Is the timing right and relevant?
- What does it take to bring the idea to life?
- Who are the right kind of people who might shape the idea to make it better?
- Who might help with the execution?
- What challenges might lie ahead?
- What are the market forces that support the idea?
- What are the market forces that oppose the idea?
- Why will someone care?
- Why should the creator care?
- Is this an opportunity?
- Is this an opportunity cost?

Very soon, one will either take the idea to grave all by themselves because it was not the right idea, or they will have the renewed commitment to take the next steps towards making this a reality.

We all know that ideas evolve along the way. Every evolution (or *pivot*, if you want a fancy word for it) is a point where you might want to stop, reflect, and think further, as not only might the idea have changed, but also the marketplace may have shifted.

Here, again, your mentor comes into play as a thinking partner to either help you re-evaluate the idea or shape it up in the new form. The mentor also can give new insight based on experience, and when this insight is added to the team equation, it shines light on the original idea in a new manner. Then others can take the mentor's new enlightened idea to market at superhero speeds.

The Power of Asking the Right Questions

The magic that a mentor brings is not in the answers that they are providing, but in the questions that he or she is asking you. Asking the right questions is like chiseling away the right parts of a rock to let the statue hidden within it emerge.

I have seen this process repeated again and again over the last six years serving as a mentor at the Founder Institute (FI). At FI, founders have access to about 40 mentors as they shape their good ideas to make them a reality, or in many cases voluntarily take bad ideas to the grave if proven to be not worth pursuing.

It happens like clockwork. Every single semester. Mentors move the needle by pointing the creators to the right resources, sometimes by making the right connections, but almost always by asking the right questions.

Changing the world – one mentoring relationship at a time

When innovation wins—be it in the startup world, or within a corporate environment—we are changing the world for the better. In both cases there is a profit boost, but more importantly there is a positive impact on the lives of everyone who gets touched by the idea.

Mentoring accelerates innovation by reducing the friction as the idea takes flight from someone's head to the real world.

[Thanks Rajesh for your expert advice.]

Chapter 10

Let's Get this Party Started:

If you are a business leader, you already know the power of mentoring and how it can foster and accelerate innovation.

Here are a few ideas to get started:

1. It starts with you

You and your leadership team have to internally believe and embrace the mentoring mindset. If you have a favorite mentoring story of your own, share it with the team. Your people will listen to you—but more importantly, they will observe your actions, so they both have to be in sync.

2. Celebrate small wins

Innovation by its nature is to embark on a journey in an uncharted territory—so the big wins are few and far between. You have to celebrate the small mentoring wins along the way to provide the social proof for motivating those waiting on the sidelines.

3. Enable discovery and engagement models

Platforms like MentorCloud will provide tools to help with not only matchmaking between the mentors and the mentees, but also streamline ongoing engagement between the two. Such tools will help you scale the mentoring initiative, and in turn accelerate innovation.

4. Get the right alignment

The foundation for a successful mentoring relationship is alignment of hearts and minds, both for the mentors and mentees. Egos have to be checked at the door and the focus has to be on the goal. As a leader, you have to educate both parties to engage with the right posture.

5. **Watch the magic unfold**

Once you have empowered your people to learn from each other, you can begin to enjoy the magic that mentoring unfolds to accelerate innovation in your organization.

Key Terms:

- **Mentoring.** Simply put, mentoring is knowledge sharing. It is providing insight and advice to another person.
- **Peer to Peer Mentoring:** Colleagues helping and advising one another.

New Roles as a Result of Super Speed

For changes to unfold, I think the biggest thing to get right are the people and roles. People can make it happen!

I'd like to introduce the roles of extreme innovation for super speed:

- **Meet the Chief Culture Strategist:** The foundation for an extreme culture is a great strategy. Having someone to watch after this culture, pivot where necessary, and work closely with a data-driven CEO is essential for the alignment of both hearts and minds for the team.

- **Meet the Guru of Cognitive Diversity**: There is power in cognitive diversity—not how we have thought of it in the past, but in the more expanded or extreme sense of engaging gender, ethnicity, age, demeanor, sexual orientation, and more. But the magic comes in by recruiting the right team, empowering them, and then ensuring that the teams work together, not avoiding their differences but celebrating them, and providing mentorship and innovative programs. Introducing a new role: the Guru of Cognitive Diversity.
- **Meet the Chief Agility Officer**: Lightning speed is essential. The Chief Agility Officer will ensure that the business processes are built to ease the business, not dictate how it is done. This person needs to understand the complexity of processes and cherish the simplicity of having the processes work for the team, in sync with the culture strategy.
- **Meet the Chief Belonging Architect**: Inclusion is part of the secret sauce of innovation. The Chief Belonging Architect is about creating an environment where all feel a part of the company. I once listened to Dr. Beverly Daniel Tatum, President Emerita of Spelman College, describe inclusion as being part of a photograph taken at a team event, but then being photoshopped out of the picture because you didn't seem to fit the theme. The Chief Belonging Architect tries to set the stage for diversity to thrive.

CHAPTER 11

Super Synergy: Customer Obsession

SUPER SYNERGY

Build Ecosystems

- ✓ Chief Ecosystem Officer
- ✓ Chief Connector and Empathy Officer
- ✓ Chief Obsession Officier

Super synergy is about ensuring that you have linked the go to market innovative approach into your innovation strategy. Most extreme innovators don't stop at the product, but continue to innovate how the product gets to the market and how customers are treated after the product reaches them and they are using it.

Super synergy breaks into three elements:

- Customer obsession
- Ecosystem building
- Connecting the internal teams

Why these three? Extreme innovators know that they must be customer obsessed. External linkage is crucial, but you cannot be customer obsessed without the right ecosystem and internal team and culture. Culture is defined by values consistently applied. A sustainable and successful obsessed culture comes from the collective knowledge derived from ecosystems that love what you are doing—both for purpose and profit. And ensuring you build the right ecosystems and obsessive culture can only be made possible if your internal teams are connected.

I have structured this section from the outside in: start with the client, then build an entire ecosystem by ensuring your internal teams are working in concert. For this chapter, I have studied and shared best practices from all industries, because borrowing from other industries takes an extreme step forward.

It sounds easy, but few achieve it.

Customer Obsession:

I am customer obsessed. The desire to know what makes my customers tick—and scream in delight—is in my DNA.

It may sound simple, but obsessing about what your client truly needs to be successful is a superpower. In the Amazon Leadership principles, one of the top values is customer obsession.[65] Leaders start with the customer and work backwards. For engineers, this is referred to as reverse engineering. They work vigorously to earn and keep customer trust. Where leaders pay attention to competitors, they *obsess* over customers.

To truly obsess about your customer means that your team understands their needs today and anticipates them in the future. One of the best examples is Zappos. Their obsession with the customer is maniacal, and this inspires a high octane energy to serve the customer with every resource at hand. Another example, the Shake Shack innovates on their experience to clients. Their CEO encourages his team to exceed expectations. They give away free custard, customize a burger, and offer to help the customer the best they can. Instead of saying "The customer is always right," they prefer, "The customer should always feel right."

In Professor Rita Gunther McGrath's book *The End of Competitive Advantage: How to Keep Your Strategy Moving as Fast as Your Business*, she writes about the change in competitive advantage, saying, "'The driver of categorization will in all likelihood be the outcomes that particular customers seek ('jobs to be done') and the alternative ways those outcomes might be met."[66] In other words, it is all about the last sustainable advantage: obsessing over your customer!

How do you capture the customer obsession spirit?

Extreme innovators have recognized three new non negotiables:

1. The company's goal is not the sale, but customer advocacy
2. The company's competitive differentiation is the customer experience
3. The company's thrust is relationships
4. The company's storytelling capability is extreme

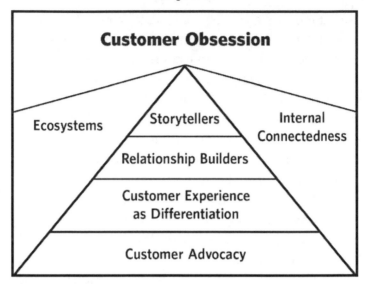

The goal is not the sale, but customer advocacy

Many contacts with customers are about taking an order (which could be done better online) or about selling the next thing. But today the prime thing that customers want is an obsessed person—a subject matter expert—who cares about their success. And these needs and wants keep changing as the bar on customer service rises higher and higher. As Waze, an application for discovering the best route, says, "customer-obsessed + technology empowered = life changing!"[67]

Innovative companies celebrate when new customers sign a contract. Extreme innovation companies celebrate when a customer turns into an advocate!

Having the team at the table—owning retention and customer advocacy—will lead to the outcome of ensuring that product market fit occurs. And that is crucial, because lack of product market fit is the number one reason companies and product fail. It's that important.

The company's competitive differentiation is the customer experience

I heard Amanda Richardson, Chief Data and Strategy Officer at Hotel Tonight, tell this story at an event. Hotel Tonight was being attacked by one of their major competitors on their efficient way to book a room. Hotel Tonight fondly refers to this as "three taps and a swipe," or "book it in 10 seconds." Since that process turned out to be replicable by a bigger, more established company, Hotel Tonight—an extreme innovator—focused on their customer needs. Hotel Tonight's superpower is that they obsess over the emotions, needs, and inspiration of their clients.

But how could they turn the customer experience into a competitive weapon and still make money? Like any great extreme innovator, they experimented.

First, they started with a new app called Suite Talk, but it was too broad. The problem was not crisp and there were too many needs they were trying to address.

Experiment number two was a new app call THX. Here they were very focused: removing the pain of tipping while supporting the hotel workers. But their clients never really got excited about its value.

The next innovation—an extreme one—was very focused; it drew on the emotional cord, and helped to establish a magical, bespoke experience. This application was called HT Pros. It was about delivering with real people—not bots—the best experience per guest. For example, when one guest said they wanted a Nicholas Cage poster in his room, Hotel Tonight asked, "From which decade?" When teachers asked about local hipster spots, the magic team researched and proposed an experience to remember.

At the 2017 SaaStr Conference, Peter Gassner, CEO of Veeva Systems, said, "Any good idea will be copied. Good execution and great customer experience is what endures."

Hotel Tonight found the way to delight. But did it lead them to monetize?

Show me the Money – Profit:

Yes—in fact, they experienced a 30% conversion rate, 47% repeat business, and 34% repeat bookings. They are now building up this small team of seven to be even more customer-obsessed!

HT PROS RESULTS

30% increase in conversion for hotels that are Pros eligible	47% increase in app engagement for Pros users	34% increase in repeat bookings for Pros users

(Revised image used with permission from Hotel Tonight)

What are some of the secrets weapons of being super synergistic with your client through obsession?

- Instead of focusing on just acquiring customers, companies focus on delighting their customers. In a Forrester survey of global CMOs, 63% said that acquiring new customers was their top priority, while just 22% said retaining current customers was their top goal.[68]
- Hotel Tonight was a nimble, continuous learning machine. They changed and learned at each step.

- Act—don't just listen. Hotel Tonight acted after listening. Many companies have ways to listen, but don't take the actions from the insights that they gain. And actions take investment. David Cooperstein, in the Forrester report "Competitive Strategy in the Age of the Customer," wrote that "a customer-obsessed enterprise focuses its strategy, its energy and its budget on processes that enhance knowledge of and engagement with customers and prioritizes these over maintaining traditional competitive barriers."

- Hotel Tonight communicated personally and proactively. The team made the purposeful decision to staff their magic team with real people, not just bots.

- They have an internal culture committed to bringing value to the customer. Having a customer-obsessed internal culture is a fundamental aspect to improving customer experience, according to Tom Champion, senior analyst at Forrester and author of the 2016 book *The Australia Customer Experience Index*.

_____

Tamara McCleary
CEO, Thulium
Client Obsession Expert

The company's thrust is relationships

We are smack dab in the middle of a relationship revolution. Our relationships with machines, and our relationships with each other, are changing as we redefine the scope of our engagement with each. We have more choice, more power, more freedom than any other time in history thanks to advances in technology offering us every opportunity to monitor our lives and everyone else's. We can locate and compare people, products, and services with a few keystrokes.

We've not only empowered ourselves, we've empowered our customers. Your competition isn't another business—your competition is your customer. The competitive advantage is keeping customers loyal to your brand, but the catch is: how do you keep customers brand loyal in a world where loyalty is directly proportional to a perception of happiness?

The ultimate challenge here is that dealing with perceptions is like shooting at a moving target. Have you ever tried to make someone happy in a relationship? Exactly. One minute you're a hero, the next, you're in the dog house. This is the current challenge for companies. It's a very real challenge paired with our evolution through technology creating a consumer with an acquired taste for variety and change. We all enjoy the freedom of having a diverse selection of options, and the speed at which we can replace anything—especially relationships—is lightning fast.

Consumers aren't the only ones who enjoy this level of flexibility, as companies are also harnessing technology to respond to rapid changes in appetite through dynamic pricing of products. Companies and consumers are living in a world of shifting sand minute-to-minute, and all of us are becoming used to existing with a certain level of discomfort and skepticism derived from our feeling into this constant state of change in our lives. Savvy companies are taking this knowledge of the human condition and are creating ways to position themselves as steady, reliable, and trustworthy. I experience this daily in the work I do, creating company personas and messaging for the social media space to build extraordinary customer relationships.

Harnessing the power of social media through genuine engagement and compelling storytelling that reaches the right audience, at the right time, on the right platform, with the right messaging, is the money ticket for business growth and acceleration. Listening to and engaging with your target audience's pain points, while creating a consumer-facing level of authenticity, is an irresistible customer attraction model because it's customer-centric and authentic. People feel you when you're authentic.

Social media done well creates raving fans and elevates brand awareness and loyalty via nurturing relationships online. People want to be able to sink their teeth into something they perceive is real and unchanging, because so much of their lives are lived in what is perceived to be a false and unreliable way.

At its core, customer obsession is understanding your customers emotionally, intimately, on a deeper level only achieved through listening—listening to what they want and then delivering support and solutions to them that enhance their lives and keep them coming back for more of your solutions, wisdom, and guidance.

To be customer obsessed means focusing on what the end outcome needs to be for your target audience. Become obsessed with how you can make their life or their jobs easier. Position yourself, your employees, your brand, and your product or service as the trusted advisor customers can count on. Begin with the end in mind. Instead of being obsessed with your own brand, product, or service, think instead about what problem you are solving for your customers.

Have you ever felt like you were being pitched? When we pitch, we are focused on ourselves and what we hope to get out of an interaction. The focus on getting something from an interaction carries a heavy energy of neediness and transaction, versus being helpful and relational. Build relationships, and make your customers your primary focus.

This shift from transactional to relational creates a subtle yet powerful shift in the relationship dynamic that is palpable to not only customers, but to the organizational culture. Employees focusing on and rewarded by creating relationships with customers are more focused on creating relationships internally as well. What we focus on expands, and businesses looking to stay relevant, vital, and growing will be obsessed with relationships between human beings.

The power we've all witnessed from social media is this precise power: the potency of genuine connection. The more we are catapulted into a future of machines, the more we all crave an increase in human touch. We want the companies we buy from and work with to feel more human, more connected to us.

[Thanks Tamara for your expert advice.]

The company's storytelling capability is extreme

In addition to identifying gaps in the market and customer needs, with any innovation, getting it out into the market is important. On the backend, innovating on how to educate the market on a new category or disruption is not easy.

You must convince your market why they should care, why this is the time for this new solution, and why it is important. Positioning happens in the mind of the customer, and it's about very simple things.

It could be something as simple as a billboard with an empathetic statement on it. At the 2017 SaaStr conference, the CEO of Twilio, Jeff Lawson, was asked about the success of having a billboard on highway 101 right when you enter San Francisco. He responded: "Don't underestimate the power of market awareness. Billboards still work!"

Lauren Vaccarello, Vice President of Marketing at Box, said at the 2017 SaaStr conference: "When everyone can use your product, it's like a marketer's dream: shooting fish in a barrel. But, here's the problem: when everyone and anyone can use your product, what you have is a couch. A beige couch. Messaging that makes sense for everyone is boring, and it won't stand out in the marketplace."

Run a mock version of your story and value proposition with customers before building the real thing.

Change the World – Purpose:

The competitive advantage today is being more human than your perceived competition. The power brands on social media have done an exquisite job of creating a feeling of warmth, approachability, mutuality-mindedness, and human connection through engaged two-way conversations, and relevant customer-centric storytelling. Notice that the brands flailing on social media have failed to become obsessed with their customers and are caught in messaging that is brand-, product-, or service-focused, not customer-focused. This will not work, as you discount the customers' intelligence and need for the human touch.

Using social media as a free vehicle for advertising and pushing out self-serving messages has never worked, yet companies flush thousands—and sometimes millions—of marketing dollars down the drain on precisely these kinds of ineffective and pointless social media campaigns. People crave to be seen, heard, and acknowledged. Build genuine, engaged relationships with your customers, making them feel acknowledged, and you will deliciously create for them a uniquely pleasurable experience—an experience your customers will come back and want repeated again and again.

Chapter 11

Let's Get This Party Started:

1. Build knowledge. As you grow, it is harder to understand how your clients make decisions and what really matters. Ensure you have a scalable way to always know your client.
2. Identify subject matter experts. Some call them evangelists. Make sure you have someone living the customer story daily.
3. Build a customer advocacy team by amazing your customers.
4. Have metrics that track your Net Promoter Score or a way to see delight—the result of a team obsessed with the client.
5. Create a Chief Amazement or Obsession Officer to help create magic moments by working with the entire team.
6. Create an obsessed culture. Champions of the clients should be recruited and trained.
7. Build loyalty. See Kevin Kelly's *1000 True Fans* for his views on keeping the social and the relationship at a level where loyalty is the objective.[69]

CHAPTER 12
Super Synergy: Ecosystems

One of my favorite jobs was when I was head of an Ecosystem team. Ecosystems are exciting networks and communities. They are formed around a cause, a mission, a product, new technology, or a variety of other reasons. The scalable ones are built on a model of win-win-win, where value is created throughout the ecosystem. Extreme ecosystems don't deliver linear innovation, but exponential innovation. However, they do require long term investment.

The Harvard Business Review states the importance of this type of ecosystem: when they work, ecosystems allow firms to create value that no single firm could create alone.[70] Extreme synergy drives innovation, as it enables you to innovate like you could not innovate by yourself.

Elevator Pitch: What exactly is it?

The super synergy of your communities of customers, partners, influencers, and employees propel you just like a championship team. There's an elusive chemistry that takes hold. These extreme innovator superpowers leverage the ecosystems to disrupt. The complex interactions and the voice of the customer synchronization is like an incredibly tuned orchestra moving at super speed. Super synergy's connections, obsessions, and partnering take on a life of their own to stand apart from the competition.

Julie Meyer, CEO of Ariadne Capital, calls it Ecosystem Economics®. She talks about the basic principles about the future:

- Consumers are driving all purchases (the consumerization of technology)
- The world is driven by networks
- This in turn makes exponential growth the norm
- Costs are strictly aligning to revenue, and everything is moving to a unit economics basis[71]

Based on these facts, she discovered in her research that the winners of this digital age are the companies who understand their role in the ecosystem and are organizing the economics for it.

It is about optimizing for the bigger win at the ecosystem level.

Extreme ecosystems:
- ✓ Embrace a broad set of customers, partners, influencers, and employees
- ✓ Create win-win-win for customers, partners, alliances, and other ecosystem members
- ✓ Accelerate alignment in the market

Embrace Broad and Deep:

Embracing broad groups of ecosystem members is a strategy for extreme innovators, as well as going deep on a particular focus, which you have to uncover by paying attention. Surprising networks of connections with shared missions, goals, and experiences can change your business.

Do you know who should be in your ecosystem? Are they the normal suspects?

Ariadne Capital chooses to invest in ecosystems around industries. For instance, their research indicated that the most profitable and suitable market for the bank was digital identity. This $1 trillion industry would enable the bank to provide digital identity to enhance its value proposition. This approach also allowed the bank to neutralize the threat from disruptors.

To explore this opportunity, Ariadne Capital conducted deep market scans of 20 digital enablers across the globe. They assisted the bank in the subsequent business viability of these digital enablers. One of the startups identified during the scanning process has since partnered with the bank.

This international banking group exemplifies Ecosystem Economics® for the following reasons:

1. This bank is a non-tech company which has partnered with a digital enabler

2. They successfully built digital revenues through this partnership and ecosystem

3. The international banking group is essentially becoming a platform, acting as a distribution highway to selected digital enablers as an ecosystem.[72]

Your ecosystem reach could be other companies or individuals. For instance, many companies are extreme innovating with influencers. When Snap released its Spectacles, a cool pair of sunglasses that records 10-second video clips or "Snaps," their approach to this innovative product was extreme ecosystem leverage. According to TechCrunch, leveraging "Snapbot" vending machines that travel around the world to distribute and create excitement, their approach to the product—from distribution, design, and use to distribution—is reflective of the cool, clever, and fresh culture that Snap represents in their ecosystem.

Combining purpose as you build an extreme ecosystem is powerful as well. Regeneron, Forbes' #3 on the Most Innovative Companies list, gathers an ecosystem of early career biomedical scientists for annual prizes and community. The award "Regeneron Prize for Creative Innovation" acknowledges, rewards, and fosters talented early-career biomedical scientists. This year, Regeneron awarded $155,000 in prize money to 10 awardees and two institutions.

I did a presentation once on being an "Open API." An API is an application programming interface. It is what allows other programmers to use a portion of someone's program. In becoming an open API as a person, I was talking about how sharing your knowledge as a person made you more valuable in today's world.

The same is true of a company. One way to go broad is to have something that enables the ecosystem to attach to you. As an ex-developer, I think that APIs encourage that passion and shared experience—and it creates a win-win-win. APIs are being used in all industries, not just tech, because of all the data that we now have available. This extreme innovation is now starting in other industries and will grow because data is expanding so rapidly.

In the publication "Hospitality Net," Clay Bassforc, Director of Content & Engagement at SnapShot discussed why hotels needed an Open API. For example, the International Hotel Group has opened their APIs so that their partners can customize experiences for other travel booking sites. I have mentioned the Forbes Top Innovator list many times, but did you know that Forbes as a media innovator has an open API?

Extreme innovators engage in strategic alliances, but they also innovate on a bigger plane with ecosystems that have shared ownership in specific spaces that are industry-, technology-, or mission-based.

Create Win-Win-Win

Ecosystems that are balanced in providing shared rewards for all members have the ability to scale and become sustainable and this doesn't have to be for tech companies only.

Tesla, Forbes' #1 Most Innovative Company, has a carefully planned win-win-win ecosystem that it is driving. Many people don't even realize the superpower they are developing.

Consider this blog post on the Tesla site by "xRadr":

"The announcements today regarding the superchargers, seem to be creating the early framework for incredible Tesla friendly ecosystem. I suspect that this will produce some extraordinary leveraged returns for tesla in the medium to long term. Assuming they can execute on the supercharger network, it will be truly phenomenal. Much like Apple's ecosystem, once you're in it's hard to ever leave. Quite frankly, Apple's ecosystem is so good, it isn't terribly compelling to leave. Apple created a fundamental shift in how people access information. I suspect Tesla is on the verge of doing this with transportation."

Many larger companies don't consider the overall impact of building an ecosystem. They see it only as a way for them to accelerate their revenue. But extreme innovators will always take the long-term perspective and build a win-win-win scenario. For example, Apple's app store drives revenue for Apple, but its partners and app providers make money as well. Salesforce AppExchange has a win-win-win strategy.[73]

Customers: pre-integrated and pre-vetted solutions are provided to customers.

Partners: Salesforce claims on their website that over 3M downloads of apps have come from the AppExchange.

Developers: With a quick and easy toolkit, developers can maximize their effort to develop new ideas more effectively. Each app is peer reviewed.

"Win-win-win" means supporting and training partners, influencers, and individuals. Mentors and evangelists make a difference here. Having people dedicated to ensuring your ecosystem success is important, especially on early release of products or even testing new features. Toolkits and easy ways to get started can make your community fall in love with you. Digital support is a huge winner here, depending on your audience.

Alignment in the Market:

Building extreme ecosystems is most successful when there is alignment in the mission and objectives of a company. I listened to and spoke with Alison Rosenthal, Vice President of Strategic Partnerships at Wealthfront, at the Launch Scale event where she showed me University of California Professor Hank Chesbrough's framework. This framework has also been used in the Stanford Graduate School of Business product/market fit class to describe the motivations that drive corporate partnerships and ecosystems.

Two dimensions are most important: the investment objective and the link to operational capability. The first dimension is the "motivation for the investment," which is defined by Professor Chesbrough as either strategic or financial. The second dimension is "organizational fit," which is either tightly or loosely associated with the ecosystem.

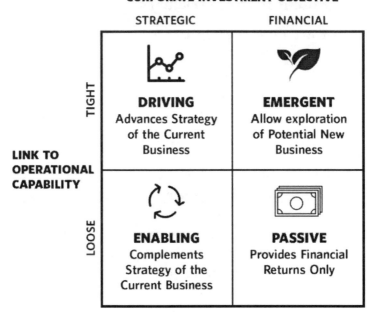

CORPORATE INVESTMENT OBJECTIVE

	STRATEGIC	FINANCIAL
TIGHT	**DRIVING** Advances Strategy of the Current Business	**EMERGENT** Allow exploration of Potential New Business
LOOSE	**ENABLING** Complements Strategy of the Current Business	**PASSIVE** Provides Financial Returns Only

LINK TO OPERATIONAL CAPABILITY

(Image used with permission from Professor Hank Chesbrough)

By placing potential ecosystems and members into those boxes, you can prioritize, strategize, and innovate on the possibilities. Unlike the 2x2 normal usage, the upper right box isn't most important. What is important is that you review your goals and strategies as you plan your ecosystems.

For instance, Facebook's acquisition of Oculus would fall in the "Emergent" bucket, as VR is a new technology, especially for Facebook. The fact that Facebook purchased Oculus and didn't just partner with them shows their financial bet on this extreme innovative acquisition.

A "Passive" ecosystem would not be considered extreme innovation, but is still good for the base business. I would place most of the OEM relationships, traditional resellers, and even affiliate links in this bucket. Important, but not as innovative.

An example of a "Driving" partnership would be Microsoft's investment in Facebook. Microsoft was trying to set a new search standard by bundling their search engine with Facebook. This partnership was all about advancing the current business of Bing.

Having a framework doesn't hamper extreme innovation. In fact, it can assist you in taking a quantum leap forward.

Big and Little Innovating Together: 360Fashion Network and Intel

360Fashion Network is a small startup that focuses on extreme innovation in Fashion Tech. They showcased their innovative product—the Smart Glove—on the CCTV Spring Festival Gala "Spring Wind" dance performance, which is equivalent to Dick Clark's New Year's Rockin' Eve Times Square show, with an estimated 1.3 billion viewers. That's right: not million, but billion!

This innovation took place through the ecosystem of a startup, Intel, and the Chinese government—three unlikely partners. The innovation was incredible. The event showcased the Smart Glove synchronizing 162 dancers' movements simultaneously to create a human light pattern. The smart glove is powered by Intel® Curie.™

This partnership worked extremely well due to the following factors:

- **Alignment:** For Fashion Tech, Anina Net, the CEO of 360Fashion Network, told me the physical needs of the glove from the dancers exceeded what they thought. She and the team had to be super intelligent in figuring out how the LED work could withstand the dance, working with the needs of the tech and the performers.
- **Embracing breadth:** The team faced a deadline and changing requirements. With the diversity of the team, the work had to maximize difference in genders, ethnicities, and backgrounds. But that's what made it so special! The differences bring out the best innovation. In a recent diversity report from Intel, it was found that closing the gap in female technical leadership representation could boost enterprise value by $320-$390 billionacross the sector!
- **Creating a win-win-win:** The 360Fashion Network team worked with the fabulous team at Intel. Without the synergy of the partnership, this would not have been so successful. Each of the partners brought their expertise to the development of the smart glove.

Key Terms:
- **Ecosystem**: networks and communities formed around a cause, mission, product, or new technology.

- **Spectacles**: a cool pair of sunglasses that records 10-second video clips—"Snaps"—to post to SnapChat. Made by the company Snap, currently sold in Snap-Bot vending machines.
- **API (Application Programming Interface)**: a way to specify how other software programmers can interact with your application.

Let's Get This Party Started:

Every great ecosystem begins with a great product, offering, or mission, then you are to have your organization create synergy through extreme ecosystems. Here are some ways to get started:

- **Foster innovation with breadth and openness.**

  Determine types of ecosystems that will accelerate extreme innovation in your area. It may be around an industry, influencer group, technology, etc. and exploration around size will be critical.
- **Create a win-win-win.**

  Culturally, win-win-win needs to be the equation. While innovating, think through the other party's goals. For instance, I love that many large companies have communities of customers and partners who directly input into the next generation of product.
- **Align for big payout and synergy.**

  Determine the categories of ecosystems and partnerships that you require. A framework doesn't need to stifle creativity—it can unleash it. Also, create a way to measure the value for each member – maybe even an innovative grading structure.

Show me the Money – Profit:

Ecosystems drive extreme innovation. Look at Apple's new app strategy that was spurred by their ecosystem. It is a great showcase the profit potential.

Change the World – Purpose:

Ecosystems of purpose exist everywhere. Girls in Tech is creating an ecosystem of developers around Hacking for Humanity, whose common goal brings them together in a win-win-win for society, the coders who learn, and the organization of Girls in Tech.

CHAPTER 13

Super Synergy: The Connections between Marketing, Sales, and Service

What is a nutgraph? My best friend wrote for a newspaper and she would always agonize over the nutgraph because she knew this was her ticket to the front page. The nutgraph is the second paragraph of a story, and it provides everything that the reader needs to know. It must be crisp and concise and packed with knowledge that you can use to impress your friends. It determines whether the story makes it to the front page.

Much like the importance of the Nutgraph in journalism, marketing, sales, and customer service are important elements of the innovation process. Although this is very much debated, including these go-to-market functions in the innovation cycle is a key to super synergy

Elevator Pitch:

Innovation is the job of the marketing, sales, and service departments

The Harvard Business Review calls it "perpetual marketing." That's because marketing's job is to look at product market fit and make the connections needed to put the oomph around a new disruption. This function is often ignored, but extreme innovation teams know that marketing and sales can help in identifying the new trends in the market, the gaps in customer value, and what potential innovations are required.

Marketing is the shaper of the conversation. Sales and customer service are points where the conversation takes place. When you ask the customer, "Who makes the brand real for you?" they will say sales or customer service.

In many companies, marketing, sales, and service are the voice of the customer—and more importantly, the voice of the future customer. But this only works when companies empower marketing to have meaningful conversations that translate into internal innovations.

Your connected team (marketing, sales, service, and more) should be the mirror around what is and isn't working in your company. Having the right product, at the right time, with the wrong marketing strategy can kill a company's chance to survive.

These extreme innovators identify the gaps, and they are curious and skilled on the solution, as well as knowing their customer. They know the product, their industry, and the company's long-term market strategy.

Extreme innovators know that marketing is more than just advertising, sales is more than just a great relationship maker, and service is more than a problem solver. They are the heartbeat of innovation. Innovation comes from market knowledge of customer needs, opportunities, understanding the key routes to deliver a given offering, as well as the competitive landscape.

Market Shifts

With the change in the market, the impetus to create and sell a product or service will continue to morph more towards solving problems end-to-end. The implications of that change are higher priorities around building and promoting community and network, and the ongoing nurturing of those relationships.

Consider this change. Products and services evolve, but the core of what needs to be understood are the complex interactions—the psychology and the sociology of how a company's offerings interplay in the world. These teams are the frontlines of discovery in behaviors—in how problems are being addressed and may be changed—where a good chunk of real innovation lies.

As an extreme innovator, you should strive to have a solid background on past trends into the same domain, but also know how and why they occurred. This knowledge provides insight to spot signifiers and indicators of new trends. After all, innovation has a huge role to play in generating sales.

In the past, I have filled the role of Chief Marketing Officer and Chief Sales Officer. My mission was to understand the complex interactions of customer value. Great innovations (such as those put forth by Tesla and Apple) arrive when the product innovator inherently understands a segment's needs, and a great marketer and an extreme innovator deeply understands their client and their segment today and in the future.

Chapter 13

Super Synergy: Connected Teams, Programmatic Approaches, and Empathy

Those top innovative companies on the Forbes list know how to gather the voice of the customer. This happens through a combined focus on connected teaming.

Consider how these best of class companies and these extreme innovators, connect teams to have the full spectrum of the market. They operate as a **connected team** with industry analyst support, competitive intelligence, evangelists, and the voice of the customer, all linked together with sales and marketing, product development, and the rest of the company.

There connected teams are crucial to our last topic of customer obsession. Internal relationships and collaboration are critical when building a customer obsessed organization.

Programmatic Approaches

To be successful, marketing, sales, and service must be involved in the earliest stages of development to help create the right product market fit. This effort involves bringing together everyone, including customers and employees, to share their innovative thoughts. Best practice companies do this in a programmatic way.

Adobe, one of the Forbes' Top 100 Innovative Companies, created the Red Box of Innovation, or Kickbox. Adobe states that the box is a "proven *innovation* process into a self-contained kit."[74]

Any employee can grab a box, learn the innovation process, and spend $1,000 on credit card to invest in their idea. There are six color-coded modules in the box to help accelerate the innovation. This extreme innovative idea helps to broaden the base of those innovating on behalf of the customer. This is an enterprise-wide quest to instill that entrepreneurial spirit everywhere, much like smaller startups have as their unique culture.

These types of programs help identify the need, evaluate the landscape, and incorporate feedback from users back into the product lifecycle.

Empathy

Innovation is an act of empathy. If your company is listening to the real needs of the customer more than they are talking, they can have huge impact. If extreme innovation is in your culture, it will be natural for teams to send feedback from the market. These ideas can be disruptive ideas, as well as iterative. Customer experience is the new battleground.

Marketing, sales, and service can be a big part of the solution. Companies that are leading the charge have tools that enable them to easily report these empathy moments. For instance, one of the most innovative companies in the US uses a tool for all its employees to enter in ideas or moments of empathy from its clients. The input is consolidated, and the people who input the new ideas from the customers are ranked and rated on how many ideas that they input.

Here is an example of an empathy moment for Baidu, another of the Forbes' Most Innovative Companies. Many of their customers were having issues with restaurants using recycled oil. They innovated chopsticks with sensors using the Internet of Things that could sense recycled oil in their food.

Marketing has become situational awareness; it facilitates and manages the interactive dialogue between the company and the amazing world outside the four walls of a company.

Show me the Money – Profit:

Determining product market fit and a scaleable way to take your solution to market are the top two areas of determining success for entrepreneurs. Including sales, marketing, and service in the innovation process enables extreme innovation on the solution and how to take it to market.

The biggest opportunities come to those who invent their own categories. Having connected teams creates the opportunity for you to invent that next thing.

Change the World – Purpose:

Communities and networks rally around purpose and social good. In 2017, we saw most of the ads during the Super Bowl around purposes that companies support with their clients. The ongoing nurturing of those relationships create goodwill and is what Millennial buyers are looking for in the products that they buy. For the new buyer, this will be crucial in the buying journey and should be thought of during the innovation process.

―――――――

Based on my Interview with Tiffani Bova Global Growth and Innovation Evangelist, Salesforce

If the intention and DNA of a company is to drive innovation, that goes a long way in achieving success. When the culture supports change and allows for failure, when the teams are aligned and the metrics allow for creativity, then everyone is focused and organized around the same goals. When companies put their customers first, and focus on how a customer can be more successful or fulfilled using their products or services, that is when real innovation can happen.

There is nothing more disruptive today than the customer. If you understand this phenomenon, you will be driven to very different approaches and decisions. As Wayne Gretzky once said, "Skate to where the puck is going, not where it has been." And this is the secret sauce. How do you determine where the puck is going?

An extreme innovator knows their sales, marketing, and customer service teams are working together to not just serve customers today, but also to determine where the customer wants to go.

Unfortunately, in most companies, there's a disconnect between marketing, sales, and customer service. Because extreme innovation requires synergy, the goal should be to move towards alignment across the board, not just between sales and marketing.

Chapter 13

Have you ever watched Undercover Boss? The CEO goes into the field and discovers new ideas that the employees knew the whole time. Why does that happen? Often the executive team will set strategy without a full understanding of the implications to those in the field who have to execute that strategy. They don't look to their own people for innovation. They don't ask customers what they really want. They don't leave their offices to see how customers actually experience their brand. Without fail, what they learn is that many of the issues plaguing the business are people and process oriented. And all that was needed was a better understanding of what was really happening in the business—not from a spreadsheet, but from the people actually doing the job.

Those providing customer services often don't have the tools they need. Truck drivers are wasting time and delaying delivery because they aren't properly dispatched. Retail stores lack consistency because each store has its own way of doing things. Whatever the circumstance, sometimes the most impactful, innovative ideas come from the least likely places.

As an extreme innovator, the key is to:
- Remove friction from the customer voice
- Implant innovation in your DNA
- Connect your critical teams: marketing, sales, customer service, and customers
- Study the best practices of the best innovative companies

[Thanks Tiffani for your expert advice.]

Let's Get this Party Started:

1. It starts with the team

Not all employees are created equal. Hire those who act like a founder. They add more value than just their job description, because they will be motivated to do whatever matters to the customer.

2. Connecting Marketing, Sales, and Customer Service

Ensure you have the right metrics and engagement models to engage these teams. Use technology to make it easier to provide great empathy moments.

3. Watch the magic unfold through programmatic techniques

Determine if there are ways that you can implement, like Adobe did, to capture ideas from your employees.

4. Use technology

Ensure you empower your analytics departments to think out-of-the-box and start looking across data sets. This will help you correlate things that seemed to be patterns. In addition, check out tools to help you capture your empathy moments.

New Roles because of Super Synergy

- **Meet the new Chief Ecosystem Officer**

  The role of Chief Ecosystem Officer is not new for most tech companies, but for the brave new world, we will see companies of all types create a role for Ecosystem Officers. The examples in this chapter alone of hotels having communities around APIs, and car companies building charging ecosystems, is a harbinger of what is to come. Define this role around the central areas that your company is betting your business upon.

- **Meet the new Chief Obsession Officer**

  Today, many companies have roles of customer success, or customer focus, or just a customer executive. Extreme innovation companies will have Chief Obsession Officers reporting directly to the CEO. They will leverage big data and AR/VR for the true "feelings" of customers and work hand in hand with the Digital Prophet to find out where the company needs to innovate to be extreme in their obsession.

- **Meet the new Chief Connector & Empathy Officer**

  A few companies on Forbes' Most Innovative Companies list have already created an organization that has multiple tentacles into empathy and connection. Analysts relationships, evangelists, voice of the customer, marketing, sales, service, and more would report into this person, whose role would be to connect the dots and ensure frictionless service to the customer.

What's Next?

We have now walked through the three superpowers and the new roles required. Next we will walk through the extreme innovator traits for the organization and person.

CHAPTER 14

Extreme Innovator Traits

I have now traveled and done business in over 30% of the world, and my goal is to do business in over 100 countries. In my travels to startups, medium-sized companies, and Fortune 500's, a common thread in innovation is always leadership.

But when you meet so many people—from entrepreneurs to top executives at the largest companies in the world—at every level from CEOs, CMOs, and CFOs to social media, PR, and advertising, you begin to observe them, and as an innovator, learn from them.

Even more so, you start to reflect on your own life. To be a leader, especially an extreme innovator, takes a lot of soul searching and courage. You are not going to be popular many times because you don't accept the status quo.

I still remember when I created a pitch competition with business schools in North Carolina. With our diversity of ideas, gaming was born from that pitch competition which we used to reach the C-suite in a game called Innov8. That game was the basis for us being named one of the top 10 games that changed the world. It definitely challenged the status quo.

The challenge I observed was how to make innovation part of the business, not an afterthought. As an entrepreneur and intrapreneur, how do you stay on top of all the changes in technology, customer expectation, the market, and more? There are only so many hours in the day.

Chapter 14

When you are a "woman in tech" in a global role, you take on a responsibility to stay true to your values and your private motivation to help make the world better, and align it with your "public why" to ensure you represent the company you work for and admire.

As many of you, I have grappled with the demands of family, living on a plane, and lonely hours sitting in hotel rooms contemplating what makes sense. Often, I have found inspiration in seeing with my own eyes those who have literally changed the world we live in today. I had the honor of meeting and chatting with Steve Jobs in graduate school, Elon Musk at one of his stores, and Sheryl Sandberg at a lean in group, Mark Burnet (of *Survivor* and *Shark Tank*) at a founder event, and too many more to list.

This is the world I grew up in and forged my career within. Yes, it was exciting to be named a top technical executive in the world. But that does not mean nearly as much to me as my desire to give back and share what it takes to be an extreme innovator—especially if it is for a non-profit, or helping others find an innovative way to raise a family, guiding Millennials in their career, or assisting others to return to work after a break.

I've laid out my thoughts in this book from my work with accelerators, companies, innovation labs, research centers, universities, and my amazing colleagues.

Leadership is so important to me that I read everything I can to continuously improve my leadership. After reading over 50 leadership books, articles, and white papers, thankfully I can say that what I have observed, learned, and experienced is in sync with the great books out there.

I took a view of consolidating from all the traits and characteristics that have proved to be the most sustainable—from my favorites like *Good to Great* by Jim Collins to *Who Moved My Cheese* by Spencer Johnson, to research in books like *The Essential Bennis* by Warren Bennis and Patricia Ward Biederman and *Leading Change* by John P. Kotter, to the new articles and research from great consulting firms and leaders. I have also studied the results of the AiNGEL assessment with a corpus of knowledge of over 6,000 founders.

Let's discuss the common traits for extreme innovators and the mindset—the private victory—I believe so strongly is the foundation of extreme innovators. As Steve Jobs said, "Innovation distinguishes between a leader and a follower."[75]

Extreme Innovators:

The six most common traits of an extreme innovator are:

- **Storyteller**: A storyteller explains the "big why." What drives the greatest extreme innovator is the founding story. The founding story is transferred to the company and the brand. Like for a ritual or a religion, the founding story becomes their gospel. It carries the stakeholders to move forward in tough times. The storyteller entertains, fascinates, motivates, and encourages. This is a critical characteristic. It falls on that line between artist and scientist. One of my favorite quotes is: "Tell me a fact and I'll learn. Tell me a truth and I'll believe. But tell me a story and it will live in my heart forever."[76] If you close your eyes and think of the leader you perceive as most innovative, I bet a story of theirs comes to mind. One of my mentors used to say, "You won't remember the decision or the act, but you will remember how they made you feel."

Storytellers touch an emotion. They convince us to take a risk with them, encourage us on our journey, and bring out our most creative side. Emily Chang, founder of Accompany and past Google Executive, said, "I never knew how important storytelling was until I became an entrepreneur. Success in these conversations is all about the energy of the connection. Smile. Be excited! It matters."

- **Intuitive and Data Driven**: Albert Einstein, winner of the Nobel prize, purportedly said that "The only real valuable thing is intuition." Combining data and intuition may seem like a contradiction, but one of the traits that keeps emerging is that both skills are present in innovative leaders who can scale over time.

I believe that your intuition should be guided by the data. Extreme innovators are people who've seen the movie enough times to know how it will end, and at the same time are creating their own alternative endings. The traits that you need to develop (or draw out) are pattern recognition, wisdom, trend anticipation, personal insight, and confidence, like you can find in Malcolm Gladwell's book *Blink: The Power of Thinking Without Thinking*.

- **Life Long Learner:** The Harvard Business Review has many articles on life long learning, and one of the quotes that I find most relevant is: "A learning organization is an organization skilled at creating, acquiring, and transferring knowledge, and at modifying its behavior to reflect new knowledge and insights."[77]

  Extreme innovators are curious and desire to learn. They learn in teams, through classes, experimentation, and failure. And they never stop. I love the story in John Kotter's leadership book about two people who are identical, except that one learns about 6% new skills each year, and the other learns 1% new skills. While this doesn't seem like a lot, imagine the difference in the twentieth year of their careers! One would have 122 units of learning, and the other 321.[78]

  But often, we learn the most from taking the road less traveled. In those moments of private reflection, ideas sometimes come to us out of the blue that could change the world, and extreme innovators muster the courage to bring these ideas to life. If we want to be extreme innovators and drive sales in new and uncharted ways, then we need "pigheaded discipline and determination," as Chet Holmes, author of *The Ultimate Sales Machine*, puts it.

- **Sense of Humor:** It may seem odd to include a sense of humor as a characteristic of extreme innovators, but being able to have fun, joke about yourself, and ease the stress is definitely an extreme innovator characteristic. I have read lots of interviews with Elon Musk, saw him present at South By Southwest (SXSW), and even met him in a Tesla store, and I still remember his sense of humor. At the USC Lava Lab, one of the people who interviewed Elon commented, "In fact, he's got an incredible sense of humor."

- **Open**: The word "open" has many meanings. It implies that the extreme innovator is open to new ideas, to failure, to other people's viewpoints. In fact, an open innovator seeks out new ideas, and wants people to debate the thought process and outcome. They build a network of people they can bounce ideas off of. Building your network is not an extracurricular activity—it is hard word, and must be very intentional. One of the top patent producers told me that she still carves out time to meet at least three new people each week.

- **Explorer:** Last but not least, extreme innovators are explorers. An explorer is someone who goes somewhere unfamiliar, who travels to places where few have ever been. In an organization, they are curious and courageous. They say and do things that are different. They are a wild duck. I was talking with a founder about how they choose their board of advisors, and they said, "I look for extreme innovators and executors. They sometime ask me questions about the future roadmap that feel a bit uncomfortable. Sometimes they introduce a crazy thought about a market, or show a challenge I had not even anticipated. They showcase curiosity and run an unsolicited stress test of my ideas and arguments."

The Qualities of Extreme Innovators

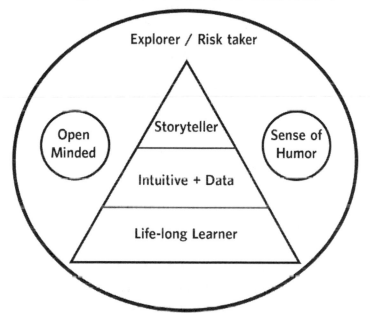

My Favorite Leadership Books:

I certainly haven't captured all of the leadership qualities needed for extreme innovation here, and if you want to go deeper then please read some of my favorite books on leadership. You can also subscribe to the Harvard Business Review, or explore lectures online from Coursera or Stanford.

In whatever way that is best for you, continue to learn about leadership.

- *Who Moved My Cheese* by Spencer Johnson
- *Good to Great* by Jim Collins
- *The Essential Bennis* by Warren Bennis and Patricia Ward Biederman
- *Leading Change* by John P. Kotter
- *The Leadership Challenge* by James M. Kouzes and Barry Z. Posner

To Be or Not to Be: When to Stop

Therein lies the question that has confronted extreme innovators: When do you cut and run, and when do you have the staying power to stick with it.

Sometimes the innovation doesn't work. An extreme innovator has to examine the results in those quiet moments when the experiment doesn't work out, and the way you handle those failures, those experiments that didn't pan out, makes all the difference in the world.

I heard Sarah Tavel, one of the members of the Pinterest founder team, explain this as a secret to their success. In her view, there are more failures than successes when you are nurturing a new idea. It really matters how an extreme innovator handles the fact that their invention or innovation is "not to be."

Michael Pryor, CEO of Trello, said at the SaaStr conference in 2017, "Sometimes it's as important to know the market you *aren't* going after as the market you *are* going after."

Celebrating both successes and failures sets the right tone, a very powerful tone that cannot be ignored.

Can I Do This?

Yes. I think that there is innovation in all of us—but it takes work. I recently watched a webinar where the speaker stated that 90% of those watching would not act on the recommendations that were being discussed.

I have two stories I want to share that capture what I think are the secrets of moving from merely reading about innovating to actual engagement and application. They revolve around acting—the true sign of an extreme innovator.

If you are not exhibiting these characteristics above, then change what you can. But keep at it. I was reading a book—one of my favorite things to do—about a person who once had been addicted to drugs but was now a super success. He said that to stop using drugs, he had to "become a new person every day." I think that is true of extreme innovators as well; it is not easy. You must practice these traits consistently. It cannot just be on a piece of paper.

While many companies come to Silicon Valley to learn about these traits, when they go back home, they often forget about them after a while. They get back to their familiar culture and processes, and soon, just like in that webinar, 90% of what they learned is forgotten or not implemented.

I am reminded of a story of the great heavyweight boxer Gene Tunney. Tunney ended up breaking so many of the bones in his hands that he was told he couldn't box anymore. But rather than quitting, he figured out how to adapt his strengths and his weaknesses. He changed his style from random hard hits to precise jabs. In fact, because he had to change and adjust his style, he ended up defeating Jack Dempsey for the World Title.

I believe that if you adapt these superpowers to your own strengths, and practice and implement them in a careful and deliberate way, then you and your company can become extreme innovators—or even better extreme innovators.

The Corporate Extreme Innovation Leader:

What does the typical corporate innovation leader look like? From the Crowd Companies research, the following is a breakdown of the current innovation leader.

Some interesting observations:

- Most have had multidisciplinary and industry careers. This aids in creating extreme innovation with multiple storylines to pull from.
- Credibility is important, and so they tend to stay in their roles longer to earn trust as they continuously learn about new trends.
- Extreme innovation leaders are not fresh out of school, nor have they retired in their career. They leverage their expertise and intuition, built over the years, with their openness to new ideas.
- The complete picture demonstrates exploration. Multi-industries, multi-disciplines, education or on the job training, and years of experience all add up to someone who is more likely to be an extreme innovator

WHO'S THAWING THE "TUNDRA?" EXPLORING THE CORPORATE INNOVATION LEADER PERSONA

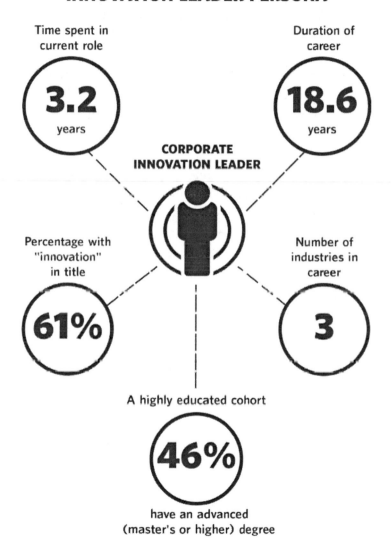

Time spent in current role

3.2 years

Duration of career

18.6 years

CORPORATE INNOVATION LEADER

Percentage with "innovation" in title

61%

Number of industries in career

3

A highly educated cohort

46%

have an advanced (master's or higher) degree

(Revised image used with permission from Crowd Companies)

Let's Get This Party Started:

- Determine an innovation education program on the six traits after your organization assessment, which is given in the next chapter.
- Do an "all-in" day leveraging the team to build momentum.
- Bring in innovators from other companies to share their stories.
- Go out into the wild to experience innovation in other innovation centers.

"The ideals that have lighted my way, and time after time have given me new courage to face life cheerfully, have been Kindness, Beauty, and Truth. Without the sense of kinship with men of like mind, without the occupation with the objective world, the eternally unattainable in the field of art and scientific endeavors, life would have seemed empty to me. The trite objects of human efforts — possessions, outward success, luxury — have always seemed to me contemptible."

Albert Einstein, *The World as I See It*

CHAPTER 15

The Superpower Assessment

To increase your chances of being a successful extreme innovator, you ideally will have all six extreme innovators traits and all three superpowers. The assessment below will help evaluate your current degree of extreme innovation, whether for an individual or a company. Many thanks to Gary Spirer, CEO of DilogR, for his assistance in pulling together the assessment that is found on these pages and online. DilogR has done assessment work for innovative companies like Colliers, and they are about extreme innovation for smart interactive content creation, personalized engagement, and analytics to build and know audiences with the goal of sales, leads, and retention, as well as content synthesis to an audience.

In the following assessment, the goal is to score how your company ranks on combining the three superpowers of extreme innovation:

- Super intelligence
- Super speed
- Super synergy

There are 10 simple but power-packed questions, each with a score from 1 to 5. A score of 1 means you are a low innovator, and a score of 5 means you are an extreme innovator. A score of 3 means you are more than halfway there towards being an extreme innovator. But don't let a lower score make you feel bad, because this book will help guide

you to find your own unique way to be an extreme innovator!

Extreme Innovation

Superpower Theme	Current State	Assessment Questions C = Current D = Desired					Desired State
		1	2	3	4	5	
Super Intelligence	Curious						Cutting Edge Explorer
	Data team						Data Hungry Organization
	Some use of tech to innovate						Organization infiltrated with those tech savvy
Super Speed	Process for incremental change						Agile process for Blue Sky Innovation
	Comfortable teams						Cognitive Diverse Teams
	Corp Culture – values, mission						Vast co-created culture
Super Synergy	Alliance and partnering team						Unusual ecosystems for win-win
	Customer focused						Customer Obsessed
	Teams focused on customers						Connected teams across customer success

Score 1 point if you answer yes to the first question, and 5 points if you answer yes to the second question. Choose 2, 3, or 4 if your answer is somewhere between the two.

Question #1:

Is your company merely curious, or are you a group of cutting-edge explorers?

Question #2:

Do you have a data team, or is your organization hungry for data in every function?

Question #3:

Do you use yellow post-it notes and some technology to innovate, or leverage technologies like AI & AR/VR to experiment with innovative ideas?

Question #4:

Do you have processes to create incremental innovation, or do you have agile processes for blue sky innovation?

Question #5:

Do you have comfortable teams, or cognitively diverse teams? (A comfortable team is one that has worked together for long periods of time, and/or comes from a similar frame of reference. A cognitively diverse team is one that has members with varying backgrounds.)

Question #6:

Do you have a corporate culture, including defined values and a mission, or do you have a co-created culture designed with your employees?

Question #7:

Do you aim to create alliances and partnerships when you have the edge, or do you seek unusual partnerships where the goal is win-win-win?

Question #8:

Are you merely customer-focused, or customer obsessed?

Question #9:

Do have separate teams that focus on customer success, or do you have teams that collaborate or even sit in the same organization pursuing and collaborating with customers?

Based on the outcome of this assessment, a determination of the places your organization can focus on will become clearer. Remember: you need all three of the superpowers to achieve extreme innovation.

In addition, there is a new startup called AiNGEL that ranks founders on their extreme innovation skills. AiNGEL assesses skills based on a corpus of knowledge of over 6,000 founders.

	AiNGEL Score
airbnb	94%
Pinterest	97%
twitter	80%
GROUPON	99%
cloudera	93%
lyft	99%

(Revised image used with permission from AiNGEL)

It then delivers an actionable report for the founder to be able to assess the ways to fill any gaps that exist. Below is my own report.

AiNGEL
FOUNDER ASSESSMENT

Sandy Carter

PART 1: AiNGEL SCORE

YOUR AiNGEL SCORE IS
75%

With this score, AiNGEL and other VCs using our scoring have a higher likelihood of investing in your startup. A low AiNGEL score does not mean a lower chance of success. It means that such founders have success attributes that can only be detected by a fewer number of AiNGEL predictive algorithms.

OTHER STARTUPS IN YOUR RANGE:
Hotel Tonight, Optimizely, Twitter

(Revised image used with permission from AiNGEL)

I would encourage you to take both the organization and personal assessments.

CHAPTER 16
Opening the Way for Female Entrepreneurs and Intraprenuers

Introduction

Female entrepreneurs and intrapreneurs are innovators. They are creating the Internet of Concrete, Wearable Fashion Tech, Car Maintenance Sensors, and Health Preventive Devices and Software. According to a 2016 BNP Paribas Global Entrepreneur Report, companies owned by female founders had 13% higher revenues than those run by men.

The estimates in a report commissioned by American Express Open show that there are 11.3 million women-owned businesses in the United States, employing nearly 9 million people and generating over $1.6 trillion in revenues. In the past decade, the number of women-owned businesses have increased at a rate five times faster than the national average.

I am so passionate about helping female entrepreneurs become successful that I worked with Carnegie Mellon Silicon Valley and Silicon Blitz on a large global female founder study. The results are designed to help female founders not just to innovate but also to scale their businesses to extreme success, and can be applied if you are an intrapreneur as well!

Many thanks to my research team at Carnegie Mellon SV: Neha Goyal, Eileen Wei, and Simrata Gandhi.

Chapter 16

Elevator Pitch: Female entrepreneurs and intrapreneurs drive innovation!

Diversity drives innovation. According to the Harvard Business Review, employees of firms with diversity are 45% likelier to report a growth in market share over the previous year, and 70% likelier to report that the firm captured a new market. But not much progress has been made in the overall numbers, and in fact, many have declined. Albert Einstein once said that doing the same thing over and over again and expecting a different result is insanity.

And change is needed. While women make over 50% of today's consumer purchases, women are still underrepresented in the number of female founders creating the products that are purchased. For example, while 64% of female founders have a history of entrepreneurship running in their family, only 6% of venture capitalists and 16% of founders and their teams are women. We need more women to step forward to innovate.[79]

Three critical areas come up as focus areas for us to conquer the female founder equation.

1. **Men have to be part of the equation.**
    - In the Carnegie Mellon SV and Silicon Blitz survey, 99% of female founders were influenced heavily by the men in their life: a boss, father, brother, or friend. More men need to be encouraging women to take risks in business!

2. **Technology Knowledge: Confidence and Competency**
   - Only 24% of those surveyed viewed themselves as having technical skills. Many of these were facing an impostor syndrome, asking themselves, "Am I really technical? I'm just an engineer." But many lacked knowledge and feared technology. In today's world, technology must be embraced.

3. **Female Founders and Leaders Must Learn How to Blitz Scale**
   - The survey showed that women have a depth of skill in their subject matter expertise, but said that they lacked fundraising skills, marketing and sales skills, and overall financial skills. These are all essential in running a business—whether a startup or a division of a large company.

Men have to be part of the equation

From quilting circles to Lean In Circles with Sheryl Sandburg, many women like to support each other. And while these groups are important and valuable (I am on the board of Girls in Tech, as well as on the advisory board of GSV Reboot), we need to do some things differently to drive change. To move to the next phase of driving more women into leadership roles in enterprise, startups, and venture capitalism, we need women and men working to change structural circles by co-creating together.

Men have a critical role to play in leveling the playing field for all talent, but they are often an untapped resource in gender diversity initiatives. Men play a critical role in supporting and enabling women's economic empowerment. Recent research highlights the significant gender gap in leadership and pay that persists across the business sector and in funding for entrepreneurs. We must engage men as advocates, mentors, and change agents. Groups like HeForShe are organizing forces just for this effort.

(Revised image used with permission from Eileen Clegg)

I have successfully run diversity groups in large organizations. Companies often ask me the secret of the success, and while there are a few, one of the biggest was bringing in dads with daughters to play a role.

Why?

Every movement must have a personal passion. Dads of daughters have the passion for making progress, as they want their daughters to have every chance to succeed equally with men. Daughters encouraged by their dads are twice as likely to graduate from high school and score higher on STEM (Science, Technology, Engineering, and Math) subjects.

By having females coding, designing, and disrupting around healthcare, safety, wearables, financial services, and more, we can showcase talent to corporations and startups, and really start the movement of change. I also have dads of daughters in the advisory board positions of diversity groups and on my teams.

For one project, I carefully selected my partner in the work effort based on his background. He was a dad with a daughter. Once I explained our work to hire more diverse candidates in tech, he got it intellectually, but more importantly, he got it emotionally. He did not want his daughter earning less or not feeling included just because she was a woman. Winning his mind and his heart showed in his passion and preparedness for our meetings.

If a startup begins with 10 people and three of them are women, the ratio as the company grows remains the same. We are going to fix the gender diversity epidemic in Silicon Valley by engaging all stakeholders. We know that gender diverse companies outperform those who aren't, so it isn't charity. And we know that if at least three of the first 10 folks in a company are women, it will mean hundreds more women when the company hits 1,000 employees.

I love engaging DoDs: Dads of Daughters. If you are a startup, start hiring a diverse and talented team as early as possible. If you are an enterprise, engage dads of daughters in your efforts for inclusion, hiring, and promotion. You will be surprised at the positive results when having 100% of the team on the field!

Technology Knowledge: Confidence and Competency

Not much change has occurred for women in the technical ranks over the last 15 years and, in fact, the percentage of women in the technical ranks has actually fallen by 1%. According to Intel's latest research, "Decoding Diversity: The Financial and Economic Returns in Tech," technical women are underrepresented by 12% in the US.

The National Center for Women and Information Technology's research also shows that 56% of women in STEM leave their jobs mid-career. This is double the turnover rate of men. The culture in many technical arenas is still very much non-inclusive.

In the female founder survey sponsored by Silicon Blitz and Carnegie Mellon SV, there were two types of opportunities. The first was for those who had technical degrees but didn't feel that they had enough skill to make it count. The study showcased that women won't apply for certain jobs unless they fulfill 100% of the qualifications, which brings to light the fact that women feel they have to be overqualified to proceed forward.

One of the interesting quotes from the survey was: "I have 3 patents in the AI area of my business, yet I default many times to my CTO when being asked questions about the technology because I fear I won't sound smart enough."

Women typically over prepare for interviews, venture capitalist meetings, and presentations, and feel less adequate in their roles, even when they are very skilled and trained. Confidence is a big factor in this challenge. Surrounding yourself with others like you helps in support and raising of confidence. There are also impostor buster classes that can assist, and simply asking for help is important as well.

When I was young in my career, I was a technical expert in an area of technology. My manager and I flew to Japan for a big customer meeting. Even though I was the only person in the room who could answer the CTO's questions, he would always wait for my manager to answer before continuing the discussion. At a break, my manager asked me if I wanted to speak up, and I said yes. He then told the group he felt sick and left for the hotel, leaving the CTO no choice but to ask and listen to my expertise. I will never forget the help and confidence my boss gave me in that situation.

The second opportunity presented is that many women confessed to not knowing enough about today's technology. But many organizations offer classes about tech; you can take advantage of accelerators like 500 Startups, YCombinator, Bootup Ventures, and more. In addition, with the advent of Coursera and other online channels, many classes are now readily available 24/7.

Don't be afraid of tech. Its power is unstoppable, so jump in now!

Chapter 16

Female Founders Must Learn How to Blitz Scale

Every entrepreneur needs to be a sales person and a fundraiser, and needs to be able to read term sheets and balance sheets. Yet, in our survey, more than 60% of female founders said they felt inadequate in these areas.

In fact, in a class that Reid Hoffman, the founder of LinkedIn, taught at Stanford, he claimed that the best startups need to learn how to Blitz Scale, and we have to scale at lightning speed. As Hoffman wrote in a LinkedIn post, "When you scale at speed, you can capture the market quickly and also outmaneuver potentially global competition. Given the parallels with military and sports strategies, we can call this blitzscaling. Literally: lightning scaling."[80]

Sales / Marketing	Business Mentoring	Fund Raising
65%	62%	65%

The number one gap that was mentioned by female entrepreneurs was lack of funding.

In the survey, a lot of founders felt that they did not have the relationships with venture capitalists, angel investors, or business leaders they needed. In addition, they felt they lacked experience with business plans to really seek the funding needed to fuel their ideas.

Groups around the country like WFFConnect have formed to connect and educate female leaders on how to seek funding and who to approach. By providing a global network and personal connections, women founders have access to capital that allows growth. WFFConnect provides a global network and personal connections. Women founders have access to capital that allows them to start and/or grow their business. This network gives founders the opportunity to become successful. With the combination of capital and experienced guidance, women-founded companies can grow at a quicker pace and increase their probability of success.

Both sales and marketing were identified as other gap areas. Filling the gap with key hires or skills of an agency were options, but many felt they did not understand enough about taking a product to market to even ask the right questions. From the Carnegie Mellon Silicon Valley and Silicon Blitz survey, many CEOs said they did not realize how much of their role was to be the lead salesperson, not just design the product. While there are many platforms online to assist, many founders said that mentorship and advisors to them were the more targeted way to upgrade their knowledge.

Key Terms

- **Entrepreneur:** Someone who starts or works for a smaller company just starting their business.
- **Intrapreneur:** Someone who acts like an entrepreneur within the company they work for.

- **Co-creation circles**: A working team with a widely diverse group which isable to bring in men and women to brainstorm and co-create solutions to diversity issues.
- **Blitz Scale:** Growing a business—or scaling—at lightning speed.
- **Founder**: Someone who starts a company.
- **Venture Capitalist/Angel**: a person or company who funds startups.

Show me the Money – Profit

Profit and business outcomes are highly favorable for female founders and innovators. Women currently control three out of four purchasing decisions in the home, to the tune of $5 trillion. And their influence doesn't stop there: the numbers continues to grow. By 2020, it's estimated that women will control 75% of all consumer purchases.[81] Women innovating and inventing solutions on the frontlines will satisfy the purchase power both today and in the future.

In the US alone, women entrepreneurs could increase the US GDP by $30 billion.[82] If Egyptian women were employed at the same rate as men, Egypt's GDP would climb by 34%.[83] According to research conducted by Illuminate Ventures, organizations that are the most inclusive of women in top management achieve 35% higher return on equity (ROE) and 34% better total return to shareholders versus their peers, and research shows gender diversity to be particularly valuable where innovation is key.

In addition, from the latest Intel Diversity report, closing the gap in female technical leadership representation could boost enterprise value by $320 – $390 billion across the sector. It is good for recruiting as well. Millennials are 38% more likely to feel engaged and 28% more likely to feel empowered when they are working in an organization that they believe fosters inclusivity.

An overwhelming majority of Millennials prefer not to work at organizations they see as unsupportive of innovation, and 40% of these same Millennials see a lack of gender and racial/ethnic diversity as a major barrier to innovation.[84]

This change is pure gold!

Change the World – Purpose

Female leaders and founders give generously. 76% of social good companies are founded by women. 50%of single women would give to charity, compared to 40.9%of single men. And women who earn more than $103,000 annually gave $1,910 to charity, more than double what their male counterparts gave ($984)![85]

Women are the primary caretakers of children. In Africa, children of mothers who have spent five years in primary education are 40% more likely to live beyond the age of five.[86]

The economy can thrive with the success of female founders, and this has propelled them to have higher expectations and change the world for a better cause.

Let's Get This Party Started:

1. Men, and especially dads of daughters, need to engage and be change agents.
2. Leaders of diversity groups, and companies big and small, need to include men in diversity efforts.
3. If you are a female leader or entrepreneur, actively learn sales, marketing, and finance.
4. If you are a company, train all your future leaders on the business needs. There is a great TED talk on the Missing 33% that demonstrates that female leaders are mentored far less to fill the gap of crucial business skills.
5. If your company doesn't share diversity data, encourage them to do so. From the Intel Diversity Research, 61% of tech companies do not share their data.

Methodology

As part of my research study, I reached out to over 2,000 female founders. I collected data from around 500 female founders through an online survey, and from over 50 founders through in-person research interviews. More than 50% of the female founders were married. I was not surprised to find out that it was a good mix across different generations. 36% of the surveyed female founders were Millennials and over 50% represented the confident Generation X. 70% of them were located in United States and around 30% of them were from Europe and Asia. As the research validates, owing to the unconscious bias, over 60% of them have at least one male co-founder on their teams. 61% of them were first-time entrepreneurs, while only 41% of them were in the pre-seed stage of the funding process.

An Interview with Adriana Gascoigne
Founder, Girls in Tech

Girls in Tech was founded with a vision around two cornerstones: helping more girls and women raise their level of competency in technology, and providing assistance for female founders in all aspects of growing a business. Our mission is to accelerate the growth of innovative women who are entering into the high-tech industry and building successful startups.

As the Carnegie Mellon Silicon Valley and Silicon Blitz study showed, female founders need tangible new skills and abilities that will result in positive changes in their economic and social communities. Girls in Tech offers bootcamps to increase confidence and skills in building business plans, determining product market fit, and finding your first client.

In addition, Girls in Tech is committed to technology for all. Our hackathons, like the ESPN, are meant to encourage girls and women who are mobile app developers, designers, and product developers to team up and have the opportunity to prototype and develop apps that visitors new to San Francisco or staying during Super Football Week could use.

Girls in Tech also does bootcamps to enhance knowledge of robotics, python programming, and more.

It is important that female founders and technologists are afforded the same opportunity as others in their fields. That's why I started Girls in Tech 10 years ago.

Get involved in innovating with the next generation!

[Thanks Adriana for your expert advice.]

CHAPTER 17
Super Powerful Advice

Thank you for taking the extreme innovator journey with me.

The superpowers covered in this book are within you, ready to be unleashed—unleashed not just to make a profit, but to make a profit with purpose, to make an investment in humanity. Extreme innovation, along with positive human relationships, combine to create the currency that drives the world forward.

To that end, you now have the mindset and the steps needed to transform every part of your life. Make sure you have an Extreme Innovator Launch Plan, including your "get ready to launch" and "post launch flight" plans, so every flight towards being an extreme innovator is targeted, exciting, and successful.

Extreme innovators go for it, and keep the following points that we covered in mind.

S	**Superpowers** combined enable the extreme innovator to move at super speeds, leverage super intelligence to see the opportunity, and connecting the dots so you create the super synergy of the whole organization.
U	**Understanding** and accessing your organization's super powers is a way to craft your innovation strategy and plan.
P	**Personal** leadership is mandatory for Extreme Innovation.
E	**Entrepreneurship** (and intrapreneurship) is a breeding ground for extreme innovation.
R	**Roles** will morph and be added based on the changing dynamics.

Super Powerful Reminders to recap of the major things needed to empower you, your company, and your team:

1. **Extreme innovation:** Innovation at its most scalable and valuable is achieved by leveraging technology, ecosystems of customers, partners and employees, as well as cognitive diversity. Ensure your goal is quantum, not incremental. To become an extreme innovator, you need to unleash your superpowers. Extreme innovators stay focused on how to grow fast by looking to leverage the smartest people who have ideas different from their own by using cognitive diversity. Once they see the opportunity for extreme innovation, like Steve Jobs saw the idea for the mouse at Xerox, they move with lightning speed and accelerate technology, ecosystem, and diversity together. Extreme innovation is combining new superpowers of intelligence, speed, and synergy to recognize, create, and jump on the lily pads with lightning speed.

2. **Superpowers** The extreme innovator's way combines super intelligence (for both humans and machines), moving at super speeds when you see the opportunity, and connecting the dots so you create the super synergy of the whole being. The whole is greater than the parts, and it enables you to disrupt your market as an extreme innovator company.

3. **Super Intelligence** requires that you and your team capture data from everywhere—big data and micro data across omni-channels, including the Internet of Things. This hunger provides new extreme innovator insights. To accelerate your insights and extreme innovator growth, start immediately to plan to incorporate extreme innovator tools, such as Artificial Intelligence, Virtual Reality, Augmented Reality, and Blockchain, to name a few. One of my recommended reads, *Good to Great,* supports the fact that great companies use cutting-edge technology as an accelerator to catapult them to dominate their industries.

4. **Super Speed** requires focusing not only on cutting-edge technologies as accelerators, but also focusing on people and culture. A culture of mentoring delivers continuous learning, and teams that have cognitive diversity innovate with lightning speed. Millennials have different connections than those over 50. Constantly set a standard of excellence to keep a new and fresh perspective, but also one that is part of your culture and DNA. Job shadowing enables a test of culture fit. Use the new techniques to get to highly targeted environments that relish speed combined with super intelligent strategies and tactics mapped out and launched without knowing everything in advance.

5. **Super Synergy** When you launch your extreme innovator approach, you won't know everything in advance. Empower the super synergy of your communities of customers, partners, influencers, and employees to propel forward like a championship team. There's an elusive chemistry that takes hold in ecosystems. These extreme innovator superpowers leverage ecosystems to disrupt and change the world. The complex interactions and the voice of the customer synchronize like an incredibly tuned orchestra at super speeds. Super synergy 's connections, obsessions, and partnering take on a life of their own to stand apart from the competition.

6. **Understanding** your organization's position is mandatory. Many companies come out to Silicon Valley for a tour, or even a three month stay, but when they go back to their country or company, they cannot adapt the learnings to their setting. Extreme adaptation is the secret key to superpowers being transported from one world to another.

7. **Personal introspection** is required, but not as a one-time thing. If I have learned one major new insight, it is that this is a daily commitment to the extreme innovation spirit. It is not a class, or even a book, but a spirit of perseverance and resiliency. Being able to understand what you need to work on to improve, and seriously doing it, means that the superpowers are within you.

8. **Entrepreneurship (and intrapreneurship)** is a breeding ground for extreme innovation. Whether you are a founder, or a company looking to partner, success in these small incubators is the new extreme innovation. This fact is why you see over 50 innovation centers from different companies in Silicon Valley alone. Trying to capture the spirit of these extreme innovators means we need to support those who have the potential but not the funding—like female founders.

9. **Roles** will morph and be added based on the changing dynamics. Extreme innovation creates new roles in organization like Chief Ecosystem Officer, Chief Belonging Architect, and Digital Prophets. Clear articulation of metrics, roles, and passions will be important and must be flexible.

10. **Join the Justice League.** Get an extreme innovation partner and/or team. In the midst of the slings and arrows of your daily lives, it will be easy to stray from these superpowers and return to the familiar comfort of following others or getting caught up in the incremental and iterative innovation cycle. Stay strong and extreme.

But that's only the beginning. Every day your superpowers are an incredible resource.

As an extreme innovator, keep quantum improvement at the top of your mind.

Come back and tell me your personal story. I would like to hear how the ideas presented in this book have come alive in your company, in terms of both profit and purpose.

Extreme Innovation

Extreme innovation is my guiding lightning bolt. It has energy and power—in fact, it's a superpower.

The experts in this book (who are also my friends) have shared their secrets openly with you, because we want you to use your newfound superpowers, as they are only powerful when you use them.

Be extreme. Use your superpowers. And share your insights with the world.

EPILOGUE

With the precision of a surgeon, the mind of a scientist, and the heart of an artist, this book was written for business leaders and innovators around the world. And the timing of this book couldn't be better.

The theme of this book is extreme innovation and exportation of Silicon Valley's model, which I have identified as the most innovative in the world. The ecosystem is all about people.

This book is filled with documented reports and ideas that would compel any company in the world to take these concepts seriously.

Cognitive diversity is a big accelerator of innovation. It makes the pivot lighting fast. This book is about a global alliance of people, countries, and companies built with a new future in mind using the principles I've outlined with my extreme innovator friends.

Naturally, this book is really only the beginning of a blueprint for the future, and the ideas presented herein have to be deployed with your new superpowers.

Timing is of the essence.

Little did I know that the timing of this book would have a profound significance I couldn't have imagined.

Extreme Glossary

- **Accelerator**: accelerators speed up the work done on startups and projects. If working with startups, they typically assist for a short amount of time – usually 90 days to six months. They offer mentors, education, and sometimes capital.

- **Ambidextrous CMO**: a Chief Marketing Officer that not only understands marketing, but will hunger for big data to fuel their customer obsession, demand AI to analyze and predict the next big campaign, and mandate AR/VR to measure customer reactions.

- **Angel**: a person or company who funds startups at the very early stages.

- **API (Application Programming Interface)**: a way to specify how other software programmers can interact with your application.

- **Artificial Intelligence (AI)**: is simply leveraging software to simulate tasks and processes that humans do today.

- **Augmented Reality (AR)**: Augmented Reality or AR is defined as a "technology used to produce an enhanced environment"

- **Big Data**: a collection of data from traditional and digital sources inside and outside your company that represents a source for ongoing discovery and analysis.

- **Blitz Scale**: a term coined by Reid Hoffman, the founder of LinkedIn. It means doing the necessary functions to grow with lightning speed. The focus here is not on starting, but growing a business.

- **Blockchain**: technology is best known as the underlying technology that makes the Bitcoin digital asset and payment system possible.
- **Bodystorming**: bodystorming is a new technique to enhance brainstorming. It engages the whole experience – all body in – by having participants create a real experience with all the items that you would need when the idea goes live – but testing out in a real environment. Bodystorming enables empathy with the customers. In addition, you can see "why" it would work, and any challenges that may come up.
- **Bootcamp**: Without any prior programming experience, basically anyone can enter these intensive on-the-job training programs, where in a matter of months you are spit out as a full stack software engineer with somewhere around a 95% hire rate. These bootcamps are in many ways a replacement for Computer Science degrees.
- **Bot**: Bots are messaging applications mostly with a conversational interface to simplify a complex task. They use artificial intelligence to drive a near human interface. The top use cases today for bots are client service and support, personal assistants, productivity, and communications.
- **Business Model Canvas**: lots of startups in Silicon Valley love the business model canvas to test business ideas quickly, and it places the value of MBA training into a single page.

- **Business Model Innovation**: this is about innovating on the way money is made. It is about creating new ways of extracting value from the market.
- **Business Strategy**: a plan to meet the objectives of the company to produce value for its customers and profit for its shareholders, and hopefully purpose for the world.
- **Captain of Innovation Exploration**: this role levels up the Vice President of Innovation role of today to the new Captain of Innovation Exploration. This person will run hackathons globally, as well as bootcamps and pitch competitions.
- **Chatbots**: Chatbots are growing in importance. They are messaging applications mostly with a conversational interface to simplify a complex task. The top use cases today for chatbots are client service and support, personal assistants, productivity, and communications. "Messaging apps are the platforms of the future and bots will be how their users access all sorts of services," says Peter Rojas, Entrepreneur in Residence at Betaworks, an American startup studio and seed stage venture capital company based in New York City.
- **Chief Agility Officer**: the role that ensures business processes are built to ease the business, not dictate how it is done. This person needs to understand the complexity of processes and cherish the simplicity of having the processes work for the team, in sync with the culture strategy.

- **Chief Belonging Architect**: this role is about creating an environment where all feel a part of the company. The Chief Belonging Architect tries to set the stage for diversity to thrive.
- **Chief Connector & Empathy Officer**: a role that pulls together analyst's relationships, evangelists, voice of the customer, marketing, sales, service, and more. This Officer connects the dots and ensures frictionless service to the customer.
- **Chief Culture Strategist**: a role to watch after the agile culture and potentially build it, pivot where necessary, and work closely with a data-driven CEO, all of which are essential for the alignment of both hearts and minds for the team.
- **Chief Ecosystem Officer**: a role to manage and drive building a group of companies, influencers, developers, clients and more into a mission based community.
- **Chief Obsession Officer**: a role to rally the company around the customer and customer success.
- **Co-creation circles**: a working team with a widely diverse group, which is able to bring in people to brainstorm and co-create solutions to diversity issues.
- **Cognitive diversity**: is about the diversity of ideas and experiences of people from diverse backgrounds, and the value this brings into a team within a company. Gender and ethnicity are usually the two areas that spring to mind when talking about diversity, but cognitive diversity is much broader.

- **Community Blockchains**: they follow the same concept as private chains, except several different entities may agree to share it.

- **Corpus of Knowledge**: a corpus of knowledge is a collection of knowledge and data that is used to train an AI system. The adage, "garbage in, garbage out" is true in any AI system. Directed inputs are critical. You need to build up the knowledge base of your AI system.

- **Customer Experience Innovation**: is about creating new ways to exceed expectations in the way a customer deals with a company or brand. Many say that customer experience is the last true form of competitive differentiation.

- **Data Driven CEO**: a CEO that leverages data (both structured and unstructured) in order to pivot, leapfrog, and serve their customers.

- **Data Hungry Organization**: an organization that leverages data to make decisions. The team is typically always looking for better ways to collect information from multiple streams of data both internally and externally.

- **Data Lake**: a repository for raw, native data.

- **Data Scientist**: a skilled person who manages and drives data in a corporation. They interpret data, combine data sources, ensure consistency, create visualizations, and communicate insights from the data. It is one of the top skills needed today.

- **Design and Innovation Jams**: a way to get a group of employees, clients, and other influencers to brainstorm together. It could be in person or online, and the goal is to take all the ideas—and these ideas may be considered crazy ones—and figure out a way to sort through them to uncover the best ones.
- **Digital Prophet**: a futurist who helps the company use big data and technology to guide new extreme innovations. Like having a crystal ball, a person dedicated to pulling all the pieces together, assisted by machine learning, will help large companies get back into the innovation game.
- **Disruption**: doing new things that make the old ones obsolete.
- **Ecosystem**: networks and communities formed around a cause, mission, product, or new technology.
- **Elevator Pitch**: a short but interesting story meant to entice the reader and persuade of the value of the topic. An elevator pitch is used extensively in the Silicon Valley by startups looking to get funding for new innovations.
- **Emoji**: a small digital image or icon used to express an idea, emotion, etc. in electronic communication.
- **Emojipedia**: an emoji search engine.
- **Entrepreneur**: someone who starts or works for a smaller company just starting their business.
- **Extreme innovation**: combining new superpowers of intelligence, speed, and synergy to recognize, create, and innovate with lightning speed.

- **Explorer(s)**: people who question and adventure into unknown territories. Explorer employees are those who challenge the status quo and question everything.
- **Extreme Innovator**: a person who is constantly looking at new methods of innovation and has personal characteristics to explore the brave new world.
- **Founder**: someone who starts a new company typically called a startup.
- **Four types of Innovation**: Product Innovation, Business Model Innovation, Operational Innovation, Customer Experience Innovation.
- **Gamestorming**: using games to prod innovative thoughts and ideation.
- **Guru of Cognitive Diversity**: role that drives recruiting the right team, empowering them, and then ensuring that the teams work together, not avoiding their differences but celebrating them, and providing mentorship and innovative programs.
- **Hackathon**: typically, a 24-hour engineering competition in which teams compete to create the best app from scratch. There may be specific challenges and technologies required, depending on the competition. Often prizes are awarded, even big money for the more prestigious events.
- **Incubator**: a program for businesses in the startup phase with the goal of promoting growth by providing resources, networking, and support for the new company. Incubators are different than accelerators, as they typically are longer and focus on growth at the right pace.

- **Innovation**: doing new things that introduce new value.
- **Innovation Center of Excellence**: this is typically in a corporation, and is used to gather and create best practices for the whole company. It's goal is to create metrics, processes, and a culture that spurs innovation inside a larger company.
- **Innovation Excursions**: taking teams from companies out into the wild – or places of great innovation – so that they can learn and experience how innovation is done outside of their four walls.
- **Innovation centers/outpost**: these outposts and centers are physical spaces and/or teams set up by organizations in a global hub, and are usually associated with a technology center. The goal of the center or outpost is to leverage the super intelligence of the entire ecosystem of the area, including startups, industry, and academic ecosystems. These focused centers can accelerate innovation by discovering new tech or waves of disruption, and explore how to take advantage of it in context. Most of these centers want to test business models, technologies, operational excellence, and more. They are about disruption, not incremental changes.
- **Innovation Strategy**: a company's plan for ensuring that their business strategy is meeting the needs of clients both today and in the future.
- **Iteration**: doing the same things better.
- **Internet of Things (IoT)**: physical things or devices and sensors that are connected to a network. IoT is the largest source of new data for corporations.

- **Intrapreneur:** someone who acts like an entrepreneur within the company they work for.
- **Job shadowing:** trying a position before the candidate is hired. Candidates are given a much clearer mental picture of what that job really is and are much more likely to stay.
- **Life Long Learner:** someone who is always improving their skills and adding new skills to their capabilities.
- **Long Table:** an ideation dinner party where the brainstorming is the first course.
- **Machine learning:** this is often confused with AI. AI is the broader concept. Machine learning is about a portion of AI that enables machines to take the data and learn for themselves.
- **Mentoring:** simply put, mentoring is knowledge sharing. It is providing insight and advice to another person.
- **Millennials:** those who were born between 1980 and 2000.
- **Millennial Mindset:** according to WorkBright, the "Millennial Mindset" is a way of thinking that builds being socially conscious into all aspects of life. Millennials pay attention to where businesses spend their money and how they contribute to society as well as what the company sells.[87]
- **Mixed Reality (MR):** the combination of virtual plus the real world experience.
- **MVP – Minimum Viable Product:** producing only what is required to test a new idea or concept.
- **Operational Innovation:** changing the effectiveness and efficiency of a company's processes.

- **Painstorming**: a technique that focuses on the customer's pain. Start by asking what pains, activities, needs, and new insights that have come up in the market.

- **Paused Career**: we encourage those who've stepped out of the workforce to call it a "pause." They haven't stopped, dropped out, or retired. They have made a conscious decision to make something else a priority for a period of time—whether that be six months or 20 years. Some are caring for young children, others for aging parents, or perhaps an ailing spouse.

- **Peer to Peer Mentoring**: colleagues helping and advising one another.

- **Private Blockchains**: they are closed for use by a single entity, be that a person or an enterprise. Private chains are useful, as they do not need to store the outside world's transactions on the private chain or demand a cost for users to store transaction data.

- **Product Innovation**: changing a product with new features or functions, or creating an entirely new offering.

- **Profit**: the most common goal for organizations is profit from delivering value to customers.

- **Public Blockchains**: they can be leveraged by anyone willing to pay the small cost to store transaction data on the Blockchain or to validation transactions for reward (usually in cryptocurrency like Bitcoins, a process known as "mining").

- **Purpose**: having as a corporate goal not just profit but social good and value to humanity.

- **Returner**: one who has paused their career and is now returning to the paid workforce, whether part-time, full-time, or with an entrepreneurial venture.

- **Returnship**: a low-risk program for both employers and "returners" to check each other out. The employer benefits by "trying out" talent who have extensive experience but may need to update their skills. The returner gets to see if the company is a fit while on-ramping their skills and network. It's a low-risk, low-cost program to let both sides determine if there's a long-term fit.

- **Reverse mentor**: having a junior employee mentor someone more seasoned.

- **Shared Ledger**: an open way to share data where two parties can record a transaction efficiently, verifiably, and permanently.

- **Sidechains**: Private and Community Blockchains in the future may become Sidechains to a Public Blockchain. A Sidechain would be "two-way pegged" to a Public Blockchain—for example, Bitcoin's Blockchain—and allow cryptocurrency to be transferred between the two Blockchains, kind of like changing dollars to pounds sterling and back, depending on the Blockchain in which a transaction occurs. Sidechains are a relatively new area of Blockchain innovation, but have the potential to expand the already large number of feasible Blockchain use cases and be a real instigator for bringing Blockchain technology to the mainstream.

- **Silicon Valley (SV)**: the southernmost portion of the San Francisco Bay area. It is known for innovation, access to capital, and a great ecosystem.

- **Smart Glove**: created by 360Fashion and Intel, a smart glove is a glove that has embedded sensors and gyroscopes in order to sync movements and gestures. Artificial Intelligence drives learning of the gestures and patterns.
- **Spectacles**: a cool pair of sunglasses that records 10-second video clips—"Snaps"—to post to SnapChat. Made by the company Snap, currently sold in SnapBot vending machines.
- **Storytelling**: a skill in marketing and branding about using stories to personify the mission of the company and brand.
- **Structured data**: Data that is in a text form and is easily organized by traditional databases.
- **Super Intelligence**: this requires that you and your team capture data from everywhere—big data and micro data across omni-channels, including the Internet of Things. This hunger provides new extreme innovator insights. To accelerate your insights and extreme innovator growth, start immediately to plan to incorporate extreme innovator tools, such as Artificial Intelligence, Virtual Reality, Augmented Reality, and Blockchain, to name a few.
- **Superpowers**: the extreme innovator's way combines super intelligence (for both humans and machines), moving at super speeds when you see the opportunity, and connecting the dots so you create the super synergy of the whole being.

- **Super Speed**: requires focusing not only on cutting-edge technologies as accelerators, but also focusing on people and culture. A culture of mentoring delivers continuous learning, and teams that have cognitive diversity innovate with lightning speed. Millennials have different connections than those over 50.
- **Super Synergy**: when you launch your extreme innovator approach, you won't know everything in advance. Empower the super synergy of your communities of customers, partners, influencers, and employees to propel forward like a championship team.
- **Unstructured Data**: non-text based data like voice, video, or picture. An example might be a video on YouTube or even a tweet with an attached picture.
- **Venture Capitalist**: a person or company who funds startups typically in the later stages.
- **Virtual Reality (VR)**: this is defined as "immersive, interactive experience generated by a computer".
- **V's: The 4 (or 5) V's**: many companies use terminology to talk about data in the form of 4-5 words that begin with the letter V. So, give me a V and let's go through them!
- **Volume** is the amount of data
- **Velocity** is the speed of the data generation
- **Veracity** is the accuracy and reliability of the data
- **Variety** is the type of data
- **Value** is the worth or importance of the data
- **We>Me**: collaboration is the future. Millennials think in terms of the greater good vs the individual.

ENDNOTES

[1] per the Forbes Top 100 Most Innovative Company list http://www.forbes.com/innovative-companies/list/

[2] https://officechai.com/news/elon-musk-receives-product-suggestion-twitter-tesla-implements-6-days-later/

[3] http://www.pwc.com/gx/en/services/people-organisation/publications/ceosurvey-talent-challenge.html

[4] http://ritholtz.com/2016/08/largest-companies-market-cap/

[5] Source: *The Origin of Wealth* by Eric D Beehacker

[6] (Source: *The Origin of Wealth* by Eric Beehacker)

[7] Quoted in John H Spencer, *The Eternal Law*, Param Media, 2012.

[8] David Bukus, *The Myths of Creativity: The Truth About How Innovative Companies and People Generate Great Ideas*

[9] Crowd Companies "The Corporate Innovation Imperative"

[10] http://www.booz.com/media/uploads/BoozCo-BACEI-Culture-of-Innovation-What-Makes-San-Francisco-Bay-Area-Companies-Different.pdf

[11] Crowd Companies "The Corporate Innovation Imperative"

[12] http://www.innovationtactics.com/author/dr-murat-uenlue/

[13] httpo://www.nytimes.com/2016/08/22/business/economy/bay-area-start-ups-find-low-cost-outposts-in-arizona.html?_r=0

[14] https://www.accenture.com/us-en/insight-outlook-california-dreaming-corporate-culture-silicon-valley

[15] https://www.accenture.com/us-en/insight-outlook-california-dreaming-corporate-culture-silicon-valley

[16] Crowd Companies "The Corporate Innovation Imperative"

[17] Here is something from Reddit - https://www.reddit.com/r/AskScienceFiction/comments/2jhdwj/superheroes_whats_the_difference_between_super/

[18] Science Daily. https://www.sciencedaily.com/releases/2009/03/090331091252.htm

[19] The Journal of Product Innovation Management http://onlinelibrary.wiley.com/wol1/doi/10.1111/j.1540-5885.2011.00851.x/full

[20] The Peterson Institute for International Economics, https://piie.com/newsroom/press-releases/new-peterson-institute-research-over-21000-companies-globally-finds-women

[21] https://www.thestar.com/entertainment/television/2016/03/28/supergirl-meets-flash-the-next-superhero-synergy.html

[22] http://firstround.com/review/70-of-Time-Could-Be-Used-Better-How-the-Best-CEOs-Get-the-Most-Out-of-Every-Day/

[23] https://www.testingmom.com/blog/why-do-kids-ask-so-many-questions/

[24] https://www.capgemini.com/news/capgemini-consulting-and-altimeter-global-report-reveals-leading-businesses-continue-to

[25] https://rctom.hbs.org/submission/sephora-bringing-digital-into-brick-mortar-stores/

[26] I highly recommend reading his article on this topic in the Huffington Post: http://www.huffingtonpost.com/jeremiah-owyang/the-ten-types-of-corporat_b_11285524.html

[27] https://hackathon.guide/

[28] http://www.datamation.com/applications/slideshows/10-big-data-predictions-for-2017-and-beyond.html

[29] https://www.idc.com/getdoc.jsp?containerId=prAP40943216

[30] https://blog.propervillains.agency/confessions-of-a-middle-aged-snapchat-user-7af2bd315c87#.kkylteni0

[31] http://www.businesswire.com/news/home/20150611005252/en/80-Percent-Business-Tech-Leaders-Artificial-Intelligence

[32] https://www.cbinsights.com/blog/artificial-intelligence-funding-trends/

[33] http://www.networkworld.com/article/3106205/lan-wan/understanding-the-differences-between-virtual-reality-augmented-reality-and-mixed-reality.html

[34] http://www.idc.com/getdoc.jsp?containerId=prUS41199616

[35] http://www.digi-capital.com/news/2015/04/augmentedvirtual-reality-to-hit-150-billion-disrupting-mobile-by-2020/#.WJoM7RA31PM

[36] http://www.techproresearch.com/downloads/research-virtual-and-augmented-reality-in-the-enterprise/

[37] http://www.digi-capital.com/news/2015/04/augmentedvirtual-reality-to-hit-150-billion-disrupting-mobile-by-2020/#.WJoM7RA31PM

[38] https://drive.google.com/file/d/0B6kDVlkzo8QyS19hOWhLWldsU0U/view

[39] https://bitcoin.org/bitcoin.pdf

[40] A full explanation of the blockchain mechanism is beyond the scope of this book, but a good start can be found here: http://radar.oreilly.com/2015/01/understanding-the-blockchain.html

[41] http://cointelegraph.com/news/115595/1-billion-invested-so-far-in-bitcoin-blockchain-infrastructure

[42] http://www.slideshare.net/CoinDesk/v3-state-of-bitcoin-and-blockchain-q3-2015

[43] https://azure.microsoft.com/en-us/blog/azure-blockchain-as-a-service-update/

[44] http://www.linuxfoundation.org/news-media/announcements/2015/12/linux-foundation-unites-industry-leaders-advance-blockchain

[45] http://r3cev.com/

[46] http://bravenewcoin.com/assets/Industry-Reports-2016/joint-report-by-jp-morgan-and-oliver-wyman-unlocking-economic-advantage-with-blockchain-A-Guide-for-Asset-Managers.pdf

[47] https://everisnext.com/2016/05/31/17-blockchain-disruptive-use-cases/

Endnotes

[48] www.theconnectivist.com

[49] https://hbr.org/2016/09/diverse-teams-feel-less-comfortable-and-thats-why-they-perform-better

[50] http://www.grnmadison.com/about/press.aspx?newsid=1819

[51] http://states.aarp.org/wp-content/uploads/2015/08/A-Business-Case-for-Older-Workers-Age-50-A-Look-at-the-Value-of-Experience.pdf

[52] https://www.wsj.com/articles/five-myths-about-landing-a-good-job-later-in-life-1480302842

[53] https://www.forbes.com/pictures/elem45igi/top-25-most-innovative-c/?ss=innovative-companies#3ac6c6e1f454

[54] http://www.pewresearch.org/fact-tank/2015/05/11/millennials-surpass-gen-xers-as-the-largest-generation-in-u-s-labor-force/

[55] https://www2.deloitte.com/content/dam/Deloitte/global/Documents/About-Deloitte/gx-millenial-survey-2016-exec-summary.pdf

[56] http://money.cnn.com/interactive/economy/diversity-millennials-boomers/

[57] https://issuu.com/mslgroupofficial/docs/the_future_of_business_citizenship_

[58] https://workbright.com/hr-vocabulary-millennial-mindset/

[59] http://panmore.com/tesla-motors-inc-organizational-culture-characteristics-analysis

[60] https://www.glassdoor.co.in/Overview/Working-at-Regeneron-Pharmaceuticals-EI_IE981.11,36.htm

[61] http://www.underarmour.jobs/why-choose-us/mission-values/

[62] https://techcrunch.com/2015/03/22/mentors-are-the-secret-weapons-of-successful-startups/

[63] http://www.forbes.com/sites/meghanbiro/2016/03/19/where-have-all-the-business-mentors-gone/#7b7b901d602f

[64] https://www2.deloitte.com/global/en/pages/about-deloitte/articles/millennialsurvey.html

[65] https://www.amazon.jobs/principles

[66] http://insights.wired.com/profiles/blogs/sustainable-competitive-advantage-is-dead-customer-experience-and#ixzz4Y4qfhCXU

[67] http://www.forbes.com/sites/scottdavis/2015/03/06/the-customer-obsession-obsession-3-brands-who-get-it/#2bf9939b39ab

[68] https://www.linkedin.com/pulse/10-things-customer-obsessed-companies-do-differently-rohit-singh-6111339685806624768

[69] *1,000 True Fans*, Kevin Kelly http://kk.org/thetechnium/1000-true-fans/ written 2008 and updated to reflect more current observations

[70] https://hbr.org/2006/04/match-your-innovation-strategy-to-your-innovation ecosystem

[71] http://www.slideshare.net/juliemeyer/how-ecosystem-economics-predicts-the-winners-62073643

[72] http://www.slideshare.net/juliemeyer/how-ecosystem-economics-predicts-the-winners-62073643

[73] https://www.salesforce.com/blog/2015/09/salesforce-ecosystem-explained.html

[74] https://kickbox.adobe.com/

[75] http://www.cnn.com/2012/10/04/tech/innovation/steve-jobs-quotes/

[76] The quote can be found in many places online. It is apparently a Native American quote. See also http://www.forbes.com/sites/paigearnoffenn/2012/11/04/telling-your-story-the-secrets-to-content-branding/#34f12db07f06

[77] https://hbr.org/1993/07/building-a-learning-organization

[78] John P. Kotter, *Leading Change.*

[79] Women Want More by Michael J. Silverstein, Kate Sayre, and John Butman, and Why She Buys by Bridget Brennan. Also see: http://www.ey.com/Publication/vwLUAssets/Women_the_next_emerging_market/%24FILE/Women-TheNextEmergingMarket.pdf

http://www.catalyst.org/knowledge/buying-power-women-us

[80] https://www.linkedin.com/pulse/cs183c-technology-enabled-blitzscaling-visible-secret-reid-hoffman

[81] Source: http://www.illuminate.com/perspectives/

[82] https://medium.com/lightspeed-venture-partners/we-support-we-women-entrepreneurship-746ddc7ad76c#.y81ktr03l

[83] Source: http://noceilings.org/

[84] https://newsroom.intel.com/newsroom/wp-content/uploads/sites/11/2016/07/Diversity_report_7.7.16_web-1.pdf

[85]Sources: 1. https://philanthropy.com/article/Most-Women-Give-More-Than-Men/159623

2.http://www.huffingtonpost.com/2014/04/29/infographic-shows-charity-is-more-than-money_n_5233390.html

3.https://scholarworks.iupui.edu/bitstream/handle/1805/6984/Do Women Give More - Working Paper 1 - 9_17_2015.pdf?sequence=1&isAllowed=y)

[86] Source: http://www.fao.org/gender/gender-home/gender-programme/gender-food/en/

[87] https://workbright.com/hr-vocabulary-millennial-mindset/

CPSIA information can be obtained
at www.ICGtesting.com
Printed in the USA
FSOW02n1353150517
34293FS